MW01006379

EVERYBODY'S EXCEPTIONAL,

INCLUDING YOU!

To MARIA -
We share our
journey of EHE!
With Love,
Suzanne

Suzanne V. Brown, Ph.D.

chipmunkapublishing
the mental health publisher

Suzanne V. Brown

Published by
Chipmunkapublishing
United Kingdom

http://www.chipmunkapublishing.com

Copyright © 2017 **Suzanne V. Brown**

ISBN   978-1-78382-357-4

Cover photograph Helix Nebula courtesy Hubble telescope: NSA/ESA/C.R. O'Dell (Vanderbilt University)

**Dedicated to Dr. (hon.) Rhea Amelia White
(1931- 2007)**

**My wise teacher
My cherished mentor
My dear friend
Thank you**

Suzanne V. Brown

EVERYBODY'S EXCEPTIONAL, INCLUDING YOU!

TABLE OF CONTENTS

Suzanne V. Brown

Preface

I am exceptional. You are exceptional, too. We are exceptional human beings. We all have out-of-the ordinary, strange experiences we can neither explain nor explain away. Actually, these exceptional experiences have the punch to knock us into other worlds. Exceptional experiences can and do transform us if we know how to work with them.

This is what **Everybody's Exceptional, Including You!** is all about. This book will assist you to better identify and transform your experiences as you step forward toward fulfilment of your life's Journey. I know this process works. It has worked in my life and for countless others who have shared their exceptional human experience accounts and EHE autobiographies with the Exceptional Human Experience Network.

People from every walk of life throughout the ages have reported anomalous experiences and have no idea what to do with them. According to several research polls and surveys between 25% and 90% of all participants claimed to have a paranormal or otherwise out-of-the ordinary exceptional experience that did not conform into the mainstream worldview.[1] For many people, these uncanny or strange experiences may be very troubling. Yet, from these sampling percentages of our Western population, we find we really can no longer call these experiences

---

[1] Brown, S.V. 1997a Exceptional Human Experience: Rethinking Anomalies and Shifting Paradigms: An Introduction and background paper, In R.A. White (Ed), Exceptional Human Experience: Background Papers II, (pp.21-26). New Bern, NC EHE Network.

"anomalous." This indicates a huge disparity in our culture. Rather than acknowledge that these experiences may be part of our overall human condition, they are largely dismissed and the experiencer is typically sensationalized, feared, ridiculed, or "rationalized" back into the status quo cultural framework.

Everybody's Exceptional, Including You! will not only help you identify your exceptional experiences, it will help reassure you if you allow yourself to go beyond the mainstream culture fears. It can help you go forward in actualizing these initial exceptional experiences—to transform and potentiate them. Further, as we begin to shift our view toward a new way of sensing, we transcend everyday reality by truly seeing with a new set of glasses. Psychologists call this way of seeing both in the old way and the new way, "double vision."

My dear mentor, Rhea A. White, Ph.D (hon.) (1931-2007) was the founder of the Exceptional Human Experience Network. .Rhea wrote extensively about how we discover double vision when we are between the ways of seeing the world—we are between the old way and the new. We can never go back to the old way after we have had an EHE. The catch is we must pay attention to these wake-up calls, ponder them and open up to their life-changing possibilities. I shared Rhea's vision of the EHE Network as her Vice President, and Director of Research and

Theory Development since its NC incorporation in 1995 until her death.[2]

Today, I still speak of my double vision and have published two books that share some of my exceptional experiences (EEs) and exceptional human experiences (EHEs). Not only have I had these types of experiences all of my life (I am in my 60's now), I have had emotional challenges and addictions in my past. So when I learned I could shift my perspective and look upon these experiences within a fresh paradigm, with a new pair of glasses, I was elated. This validation was a tremendous leap forward for my overall body-mind-spirit health and getting on with my life.

Rhea and I identified five stages of transformative growth of the EHE process:

- Stage 1: The Initiating Event/ Experience;
- Stage 2: Search for Reconciliation;
- Stage 3: Between Two Worlds;
- Stage 4: In the Experiential Paradigm;
- Stage 5: A New Way of Being in the World.

Later in 2000, I identified twelve milestone markers that belong with each of the stages, and created a 5 X 12 matrix map. This map made it easier for experiencers to identify themselves and their progress. For example, I used to have

---

[2] Rhea incorporated the EHE Network in North Carolina soon after moving to NC in 1995. EHEN was also incorporated in NY in 1995 soon before she moved, as it was an offshoot of her Parapsychology Sources of Information Center (PSI Center), which was first incorporated in NY in 1983.

alarming visions of events that happened before they happened (this is called "precognition" by the parapsychologists). I thought I was going crazy. I knew that medical doctors, mainstream psychologists and other traditional authorities on mental health would probably agree, as I had a Ph.D. in psychology and had been entrenched for many years in what was considered "normal." The experience itself crosses over some personal threshold of normal and therefore I *questioned whether I was normal.* That fear of not being normal is the hallmark of Stage 1. In Stage 2, I went on a book-buying spree, and visited many workshops and psychics during the 1970s/1980s searching to better understand that "underground" of New Age gurus, shamans, alternative religions, academic parapsychology and other optional ways of looking at my experiences.

It was in Stage 3 when I finally realized that no one else—no specialist, no guru, no shaman, no psychic—had my answers. I had crossed into the land of double vision, realizing it was up to me to go forward. I had begun an inner paradigm shift where I could slide back and forth in both the old reality way and the new reality way of thinking and being. By then, I had addressed the precognitive visions from many angles and the search had changed me. I could never go back to the tight, conformist way of perceiving my exceptional experiences, the world and my place in it. I had to go forward—I felt pushed to move on.

It is in Stage 4 when we pay attention to our exceptional experiences (EEs) and activate them. Our EEs then become *humanized*—they become exceptional human experiences (EHEs). We internally shift the EE and the EE shifts us. This is the internal, transformative process at Stage 4. It is a seemingly miraculous process. We may either jump directly into Stage 4 (such as through a near-death experience or a spiritual "rebirth") or we can shift gently into it from Stage 3.

The EHE Process is not necessarily a linear, forward moving sequence. The keynote of Stage 4, in the Experiential Paradigm, is *knowing* for oneself that All is connected—that time and space boundaries are only human-made constructions. We are the *More* of who we are. Being in the experiential paradigm often is expressed simply as "Home" or a place that houses one's essence or essential spirit—the soul.

For me, I realized at this point I was on a life Journey. It was with my cosmic consciousness revelation one day, hiking in the Blue Ridge Mountains of Virginia, that I suddenly *knew* there were no divisions or separations; paradoxes do not exist. It/We (God, Source, Higher Power, quantum physics) is/are all One connected consciousness. We are all one song— the Uni-verse. I knew I had crossed into another dimension of being, I had transcended the old way of being in the world. I hungered to hold on tightly to that cosmic experience. I was then an EHEer.

In Stage 5, a New Way of Being in the World, I was pushed by these EHEs to find fresh meaning in my life; to discover or try to uncover some of my reasons for being on this earth at this time. This is an extremely intense experience all of its own. For me, I find synchronicities, those meaningful coincidences, let me know when I am "in the flow" of universal alignment. From my point of view, synchronicities are milestones along my Life's Journey. I believe sharing this book is part of my reason for being, too, at this time. For now, suffice it to say, we are living a life-long process of profound growth that can begin simply with one exceptional experience.

Everybody's Exceptional, Including You! Includes a Dictionary of Related Terms—An Experiencer's Guide in Appendix I, should you need further definitions of some of the EE/EHE-related terms. Appendix II identifies over 400 types of exceptional experiences. Examples from my own history and accounts others have shared with me are sprinkled throughout this book to illustrate points.

The lingering question remains, "How can we take a simple meaningful EE, such as a coincidence, and grow it into lifetime serendipity?" I share some examples of this process in *Everybody's Exceptional, Including You!* After all, you can probably say you have had at least one meaningful exceptional experience. The challenge is, how can we shift the EE into an EHE? I feel confident you will discover how your own exceptional experiences and exceptional human experiences move you toward your higher calling in life. Exceptional human experiences have the power to remind us of where we have been and where we are going. Exceptional human experiences change lives and set us on our continued path or a new path we may have only "forgotten." I truly hope *Everybody's Exceptional, Including You!* becomes an exceptional human experience for you!

Suzanne V. Brown

Chapter 1
Views on Exceptional Experiences and a Self Quiz

Have you ever had an exceptional, out-of-the ordinary experience you could not explain or explain away? Have you ever had a déjà vu, meaningful coincidence or been "in the zone?" What about an out-of-body or near-death experience? Or, has your experience been somewhere in between common to rare, such as seeing shimmery lights, knowing something is going to happen beforehand or communicating with others using only your mind? Exceptional human experiences mark milestones on our life's Journey. For example, what do you do when you are suddenly confronted by a dream that comes true or a cosmic revelation? It is these types of exceptional experiences (and over 400 more) that have the intrinsic power to catapult us into other ways of being, doing, living and *knowing*—if we acknowledge them and follow their lead.

These are a few of the over 400 types of exceptional experiences (EEs) Rhea A. White and I catalogued in our work with the Exceptional Human Experience Network. I will share stories in Chapter 3, but suffice it to say at this point most all adults have experienced and reported at least one unusual EE that has caused them to pause and take notice.

Just one day's look at the popular media, the TV shows and mainstream articles, devoted to haunting, ESP, searching for Big Foot, UFOs, and so on indicates we are curious about others' experiences and about our own. However, many of these popular paranormal stories are coming from the creative minds of writers and are either grossly exaggerated or simply untrue. The TV viewer or reader can easily become confused as to what is real and not. Yet, you, personally, had a strange experience. You may have wondered about it. It may still make you curious. You ask yourself whether it was true or was it unreal. You are not alone.

The fact is, more people than ever are reporting exceptional experiences. We may ask, "Am I losing my mind?" Being concerned and afraid of our experiences typically marks the first stage of the EHE process.

When I talk casually with friends and colleagues about exceptional experiences, it never seems to fail that they have a story to share about an experience or two. Often it takes a bit of time for the person to open up. In general, people need to feel safe, before they can share. I encourage them and perhaps tell a story of mine to reassure them. Then, their account often comes tumbling out. I am at times stunned by the emotional depth and concentration of the exceptional experiencer (EEer) when telling the story. There is no doubt to me that the EEer is, at some level, reliving the experience again in current, real time.

I mentioned earlier that surveys show that as many as 90% of participants report an EE of some type. For example, one study that is easily accessible on the web is Rosemary Breen's

ongoing survey.[3] Initially, Breen conducted a
survey of 3100 participants and reported her
results in 2011. (Her study continues today, asking
on-line participants to note their paranormal
experiences.) She found that survey responders
reported experiences which ranged from
commonly reported déjà vu's to more rarely
reported near-death experiences and many types
in-between such as premonitions (knowing
something is going to happen before it happens),
apparitions (ghosts), telepathy (mind-to-mind
communications), out-of-body experiences, and
mind-over-matter (levitation, remote healing, and
so on.). Déjà vu is by far the most common EE
according to Breen. Eighty-five percent of survey
participants reported this EE in the Breen survey.
Déjà vu often causes a person to pause, to stop
and ask: *Have I been here before?* And try hard to
remember: *What happens next?*

When I was about eight years old, I visited
my friend Judith's comfortably furnished home for
the first time. I was going to her birthday party.
She lived about a mile away. I walked into Judith's
home through her front door and saw stairs in
front of me, leading up to the second floor. I was
immediately dumbstruck and off-balance: I had
been here before! I searched my memory: When
and where had I been here before? What happens
next? The memory came tumbling out in an
instant. I saw in my memory a bare house with no
furniture, and people moving boxes out the door. I
saw the stairs *in this memory*. What happens

---

[3] Rosemary Breen's website with her survey is easily accessed on
the web: www.PsychicRevolution.com.

next? I (floated?) up the stairs and saw rooms with a few boxes on the floor and each room's windows. I had no idea what I'd just experienced—to remember the bare house, when I had never been to that house before was quite a shock!

Later that evening I excitedly asked my father about this strange experience. He said this is called déjà vu. He said that déjà vu is like a flash of remembering which is triggered by being at a location or in a circumstance that all of a sudden feels strangely familiar. The key is to ask what happens next and work with the déjà vu; you may actually find a sequence of events which follow the familiarity. This was one of the very first talks about the "strange stuff" I was to have with my father during our few years together.

You could call my story of déjà vu also a meaningful coincidence. For me, meaningful coincidences, also called synchronicities, are very common. I continue to wonder about them because some have been so powerful they have changed my life. Others make me laugh out loud, such as thinking of a song and then turning on the radio to hear that very song! I was the Editor of a column, "Synchronicity Connection," in the newsletter *EHE News* for several years. During that time, I published incredible stories of synchronicity.

One remarkable instance involving me was when my father first met my mother's family in Oregon in 1950. He was telling his future in-laws about holding German prisoners of war in a Southern U.S. POW camp after WWII before they could be sent home. My father explained there was a remarkable young German, named Henry, who had a beautiful singing voice and would entertain everyone at the camp—U.S. soldiers and German soldiers alike. Henry's voice was soothing; he was in demand. Listening to the story, my mother gasped, as did her parents. You see, Henry was my grandfather's nephew! Such a coincidence! This story has a happy ending: Shortly thereafter, Henry came to America to work and was sponsored by my grandfather until he became a U.S. citizen. This story still has the power to awe me. What were the chances of my father's future father-in-law being the uncle of this German singer my father knew and remembered so well?

Before we go any further, I would like you to take a short self-quiz. You are now your own expert. This twenty question "YES/NO" quiz will help you better understand your own views on exceptional experiences. You may also begin to see patterns in your own types or classes of experiences. Let's see how you do:

1. Have you ever had an experience that you could not explain or understand?
2. Do you think there is more to the world than understood with the five senses?
3. Have you ever felt you were not connected to your body?
4. Have you ever played sports far above your "normal" scores or ability?
5. Do you sometimes remember events from the past out of the blue?
6. Have you ever communicated with someone using only your mind?

7. Have you ever experienced "missing time"?
8. Do you have vivid dreams that seem very real after you awaken?
9. Have you had any dreams or visions that came true?
10. Have you ever sensed someone in the room and no one is there?
11. Did you ever see lights, shimmering or in balls, with no apparent source?
12. Have you seen white or colored lights surrounding a person or animal, or even a plant?
13. Have you ever had one or more sudden life-changing events?
14. Do you think of a person and then that person phones, texts or emails?
15. Have you changed your life direction based on a meaningful coincidence?
16. Do you sometimes hear music when you see color or vice versa?
17. Have you ever experienced a sense of nostalgia for the early days?
18. Have you ever encountered an uncanny, inexplicable or weird thing or being?
19. Did you ever feel that everything is connected?
20. Do you sometimes believe you have been reborn or awakened to a new reality?

If you answered even one question "YES," you are an exceptional experiencer (EEer). And, as the experience becomes a milestone, a memory in your life, it is in some way acted upon. If you have undergone this inner shift, then you have *potentiated* it. Your experience then becomes an exceptional human experience (EHE) and you are an EHEer.

Let us go through the list for some discussion. Which questions did you answer "YES" to? Which were answered a definite "NO"? Were there any instances where you were not sure about their value? I have been unsure about some of my experiences—I have questioned whether there were "real" or not. Now, a secret to developing your savvy in understanding your EEs/ EHEs is *not* to question whether the experience was "real" or not. Rather, if you had your experience, then no one else is your "expert." *You* are your own expert on your own experience, no one else. You were there; no one else was inside you. This is a major key to moving forward in your transformative growth to a higher, deeper, personal, evolutionary progression. We will cover the EHE process in depth later in Chapters 4 & 5. For now, let us move on to the questions.

Question 1 asks whether you have had any exceptional experience at all. This sets the stage for the rest of the questions. Any YES to any of the following questions would indicate a YES to this first one as well.

Question 2 looks a little into your belief system—your philosophy of life. How do you access your world? Is your world more than what you would normally perceive with the five senses of seeing, hearing, tasting, smelling and touching? Do you sense other things, beings, colors, sounds, and so on, as a way of perceiving that which is not "normally" considered coming from your five physically known senses? If this is so, you may have experienced some extra-sensory perception (ESP).

Question 3 is about an out-of-body (OOB) experience. For example, an OOB may occur when a person undergoes a traumatic car accident and then watches the paramedics rescue him or her. You might even think my déjà vu experience earlier in this chapter *could have been* an OOB experience because I "visited" Judith's house sometime when no one was living there. I recall *floating* up the stairs and looking at the vacant rooms from a "taller" perspective than that from the height of a short, eight year-old girl. Another form of feeling unconnected with your body is when you may have simply dissociated away for a time. For example, you may have watched yourself giving a lecture as if you were sitting in the first row of the classroom. It is as if you are on the outside looking in. Or, you may have been driving a car and not remember how you got to your destination.

Question 4 asks whether you have ever been in the sports *zone*. One time when I was playing tennis, the ball seemed to slow down so much I was able to get to it easily and hit it accurately in plenty of time. On that day I won the neighborhood tennis club tournament. Another time I was bowling and it just seemed so easy. My average was 136 during those days and on that particular day I bowled over well over 200!

Question 5 gets at our strength of memory for events that have been hidden or forgotten, yet pop up just when we need them, or we surprise ourselves with some knowledge we did not know we had. Another form of this is when we all of a sudden envision, or sense, ourselves from another time or place we've never been in, at least in this lifetime. This question digs at the topics of reincarnation, memory, and déjà vu. It is a question to cause pause.

Question 6 involves telepathy. Have you ever communicated with someone, including a pet, using only your mind? How did you know? I have had a couple of experiences where I "heard" a person on the opposite coast of the US "call" me for help. In both instances the person was n dire straits and I recall the depth of their fear. That must have been what connected us. It seems a strong emotion or bond, such as that between a mother and child also, has a lot to do with contacting that person via telepathy.

Question 7 asks about "missing time." Some experiencers in our database had no recall of events until suddenly reminded of them, such as through a flashback or hypnosis. I have a longtime friend who told me she was driving to her house two hours away when all of a sudden she saw a blinding light. She only remembered seeing the blinding light after she found herself parked on a strange road a mile or two from her home, but not at her home. Somehow she had made the trip in less than twenty minutes! Where did the other hour and 40 minutes go?

Question 8 gets at the topic of vivid and lucid dreaming. Do you remember those times when you awakened from a particularly vivid dream? How difficult it was to shake off because it felt so real? Or, even more so, do you recall being *inside* of the dream still sleeping and *knowing* it as it is still taking place? These types of dreams are called "lucid dreams."

Question 9 concerns having any dreams or visions that came true. These do not necessarily relate to major disasters or prophecies. For example, you see a vision of apples and your friend drives you to an apple orchard later that day. Such instances could be considered not only precognitive experiences but also synchronicities as well.

Question 10 gets to the topic of apparitions or ghosts. In particular, some people who are still grieving over a loved one's loss may feel a touch or smell of a familiar cologne, or hear a voice when no one else is in the room. My colleague and friend Dianne Arcangel has written extensively on this subject. In fact, her book, *Afterlife Encounters*[4] is a gem of reassurance and comfort to those grieving over lost loved ones. Yet, this question of sensing someone when no one is present may happen whether you are grieving or not. The main point is there are different ways of sensing besides "seeing" when it comes to things that go bump in the night!

Question 11 reflects on lights with no apparent source, such as glowing balls that bounce or glide around the room. Or, perhaps you have seen shimmers of light? A good friend of mine, when I lived in Richmond, Virginia in the early 1980s, told me he saw two balls of white light gliding along the walls of his bedroom one night. These lights left

---

[4] (2005) Arcangel, Dianne. *Afterlife Encounters: Ordinary People, Extraordinary Experiences*. Hampton Roads Publishing Company, Inc.; Newburyport, MA.

him in a quandary--where were they from and what were they? I have heard similar stories, but this was the first time a friend had shared that type of experience with me.

Question 12 is about sensing auras. Try this activity to see if you can see your aura now: Put your arm or hand against a white or light-colored wall. Next, soften your gaze; let your eyes defocus. Now, look at your bare arm or hand for a minute with your defocused eyes. Do you see light around your outstretched arm or hand? If you do, then you are seeing its aura. For fun, try this when a friend is sitting across from you against a neutral background. I have found that this method of softening or defocusing my eyes gives me a high level of skill in aura detection. Hope you were able to do this, too!

Question 13 asks you to reflect on any life-changing events. What were the major turning points in your Journey? When we get to Chapter 9, this recall of your life's milestones will be essential to outlining and writing your own EHE autobiography. You may very well see that it was an exceptional experience transition to an exceptional human experience that moved you to change your life path.

Question 14 is another way of getting at synchronicity and/or telepathy. When I think of a person after no contact for a long time and then she contacts me, I am flabbergasted! As I wrote earlier, sometimes it is an extreme tie of emotion that reconnects people after many years. Yet, this time you may have simply been thinking about someone, and then that person reaches out. This is similar to Question 6, however, there is a subtle difference: It "feels" as if there is almost a causal relationship where we first think of the person and then she contacts us. I do not know which is more stunning—being contacted by my friend out-of-the blue or thinking of her out-of-the-blue and then she calls. Probably both!

Question 15 asks whether you have had a major twist in your life based upon a meaningful coincidence, or synchronicity. When you get a new job or suddenly move to a new city or find a surprising new relationship in your life, it is often considered serendipitous. These are fun, because we may see them as acts of Grace or Providence, too. They are often considered awesome gifts coming "just in time."

Question 16 is about the perception of "synesthesia." Synesthesia is when we crisscross our five senses. I may *see* music or I may *hear* colors. For example, think about the movie *Fantasia.* Do you remember during the very first part, when the background *music splashed different colors* on the screen as you were *hearing* Bach's *Toccata and Fugue*? Fantastic experience! This is how a person with synesthesia of music and color might perceive. My dear friend Nancymarie used to tell me she would "touch" an old wall and "see" scenes or "hear" voices from past ages. Nan was also doing a form of what parapsychologists call "psychometry." Yet, for sake of simplicity here I find these two terms, *synethesia* and *psychometry* related cousins.

Question 17 asks about nostalgia. When we remember our past or parts of the past fondly, sometimes we are in a deeper state of being than ordinary wakefulness. Personally, I often wonder why these former experiences tug on me so. Perhaps it is because I must not let them go. They are, perhaps, EEs waiting to be potentiated, transcended and transformed into EHEs. They are a great starting point in writing your EHE autobiography!

Question 18 asks about far-out encounters. From unidentified flying objects (UFOs) to ghosts to Big Foot to little gray humanoids, we are stopped in our tracks, faced with such mystery. I now live in the Phoenix area. Often unexplained lights in the night sky are abundant here. I have seen large shimmering white orbs in the night sky on three separate occasions. Then, after ten minutes or so, they suddenly disappeared. On another occasion, I saw a huge reddish-orange fireball moving slowly across the night sky. After ten minutes or so, it, too, vanished into nowhere! Awesome!

Question 19 goes into the inner, moving experience of "cosmic consciousness" or "mystical awareness" where you may find All is connected—there is no time and no space, and everything is in relation to everything else. That feeling is one I go back to when I feel worried or lost. These types of experiences help me know that I am not alone in the grand scheme of things.

Question 20 speaks to spiritual rebirth or a mystical (not necessarily religious) awakening after what feels like a long slumber. By Stage 5 in the EHE process, we discover a New Way of Being in the World. We act upon the world with our newfound, more connected EHEer self. We have been reborn into a new way of life by transcending the basic experience to potentiate it.

So, now look at your original YES/NO answers and compare them to what you have learned from the brief descriptions. Do you think you have had more EEs/EHEs than originally thought? Did you change some NO's to YES's? Sometimes all it takes is an explanation before we can agree to something that once seemed odd or foreign. At first, I had a difficult time admitting to myself or anybody that I had any of these types of uncanny experiences. Now I can honestly say I have had most of them. Sometimes we simply need to feel it is okay. Sometimes we simply need to be authentic. This, too, is part of our EHE process.

In the next chapter, I will share some secrets on how I have learned to "bring in and accept" my experiences. Although there are many books available on the market for meditation and relaxation and mindfulness, I want to share some personal keys with you from what has worked for me and other EHEers. I will give you a clue: I do not meditate by "blanking out" my mind.

Chapter 2
In the Flow of Growing Awareness

In Chapter 1, you took a self quiz. That quiz was to get you thinking about the different types of exceptional experiences you've had. How do you feel now about your life experiences? What about those odd, unusual, to downright freaky events? Do you now feel more comfortable learning that you are not alone? Remember those surveys showing up to 90% of the people asked have had some sort of exceptional experience? You will read later in this book that the type of EE itself is not as important as the process and the inner changes you undergo. Any type of bizarre experience may have the power to shift your perspective--to throw you into double vision and beyond.

In this chapter, I will often use synchronicity as a category of experience where our awareness shifts from ordinary waking attention—the busy, everyday "to-do" life—to the extraordinary—the "being in the flow" life. How does this shift occur? Why do some people get into the flow of Universe easily and others seem to be constantly battling barriers and brick walls?

The use of the "flow" metaphor is defined here as a "natural, effortless unfolding of our lives in such a way that we are moved toward wholeness and harmony"[5]. The flow concept helps us envision this forward-shifting, sometimes even

---

[5] (1990) Belitz, Charlene & Lundstrom, Meg. *The Power of Flow: Practical Ways to Transform Your Life with Meaningful Coincidence.* Three Rivers Press, NY, NY.

actively propelling, motion toward significant milestones on our Journey. The flow is not a goal in itself; it is a process that never ends. Yet, each time we enter it, by widening our awareness, we sense we are indeed getting closer to our true Purpose. It is an inner feeling often triggered by outer events. The outer event and the inner awareness come together as Aha! moments. When we are in the flow, synchronicities happen—Aha!'s occur.

So how do we attain more such moments in our life? How do we enter the flow?

Do you recall the short experiment you did to better understand auras in Question 12? That task took only a few moments in which you defocused and softened your eyes. In some way, because you did this, you were *focused* on your task. The "rest of the world" became silent at that moment. This is an odd paradox: You were not focused with your eyes, yet you were focused directly on what you were seeing and doing, so much so the world was tuned out. You "saw" something that is not "normally" seen with the five senses. This paradox is a major key to widening awareness coming in through any of the senses and beyond.

Here is another example: Suppose you are lost in the woods. You see a bird fly overhead just when you are despairing. You see (a focus) the bird fly to your left and *at the same time* you get an awareness, a feeling inside, a hunch, an intuition (a defocus) to follow the bird's lead *for no apparent reason* and take the left path through the woods. You walk and within a short spell you find a larger path. That path quickly leads to a town, where you not only find a ride back to your car, you find a person who becomes a very special in your life. You went with a hunch, an intuition; you followed and "listened" to your inner wisdom. You tuned out the fear and let the flow come through by something as seemingly simple as focusing on a bird's flight! The bird was a focus; the intuitive connection was your defocus. The result was a serendipitous meeting with a soon-to-be lifelong friend.

When have you felt you were in the flow, following your hunches, your intuition? Now, I am not suggesting running willy-nilly rampant and following every thought or feeling that comes your way. That could be dangerous. The key here is to have a focus and within that very moment take your awareness, your flash of insight, and discern whether the connection feels correct. For me, I recognize warmth inside my center of being and a *knowing* that the outer event and the inner awareness are connected—they are synchronous. Yet, paradoxically again, being in the flow is not necessarily marking a close connection in time; it may be a connection *based totally on meaningfulness. It could also be many years before it strikes you as an Aha!*

For example, I recently attended a seminar about Carl G. Jung's archetypes here in Phoenix. Simply defined, archetypes can be envisioned as the different personalities we wear or as representing the different stages or situations of our lives as we travel on our Journey. A few examples of archetypes from Jung are the Hero, the Wise Old Man, the Earth Mother, Star-Crossed

Lovers, and Death/Rebirth. The speaker shared some of these key major milestones of the archetypal Journey. During the presentation, something he said brought me back to the mid-1980s. You see, he reminded me of some deeper connections to synchronicity, Jung, and some ancient forms of divination. He reminded me Jung said that in divination we receive the exact answer we are meant to receive at that exact moment we ask our question. When the speaker was discussing this, a flood of memories came back to me.

Now, you must know something further about my background. I had two ways of looking at synchronicity: in my past, I used to "read" tarot cards, figure numerology numbers, and throw the I Ching coins for hints into the future. These are some examples of divination. On the other side, I used to scientifically study the works of Jung and synchronicity. In the 1980s, I did not know that Jung and divination were related in any way. I was just getting my feet wet with some alternative ways of thinking because of some of my vivid precognitive dreams. Yet, I still described myself as being a hardcore scientist. To me, the tarot was for fun, for entertainment.

It would not be until the 1990's when I learned through reading more of Jung's works that he saw the association of divination results as a form of synchronicity. Jung theorized that divinations, such as throwing a pattern sequence of three I Ching coins, were synchronistic—a causal and timely "answers" for the questioner. Although Jung did not seem to use the tarot, he did speak of archetypes, which are hallmarks of the major cards of a tarot deck, and wrote of the synchronicity of divination in general.

The point of this story, however, is that by my being at that particular seminar in early 2015, a rush of Aha's! came to me. The converging dynamic of the outer event of the seminar discussion *about synchronicity* with my inner, meaningful *connection—thus, a synchronicity about synchronicities—gave* me a laugh. That seminar about synchronicities conjured milestone memories of the past.

Plainly said, on that day I was at the right place at the right time for the right reason. I was excited to have been there and have all those memories come back to me—to see in hindsight just how far I had gone on my Path. I felt I had transcended my old ways of viewing divination over the years. I *knew* within myself that there was a connection between divination results and synchronicity. *Yes, I had read it in books, but this was now an inner knowing.* When did I know? I'm not sure, yet I knew I had reframed my thinking the moment the connection hit me at the seminar.

To return to exceptional experiences: When you begin to find meaning in your individual experiences, you find meaning in your whole life. Rather than life being a series of battles and brick walls, it becomes full of joy and purpose. No longer do we selectively attend to our problems individually, narrowing our focus. Instead, we open up, widen our camera aperture, so to speak, on what is going on around us. Many times this leads to a very subtle sensing. It may take a bit of work, but as with seeing the aura of light around your arm or hand or people, the little bit of work can pay off. The flow of exceptional experiences such as synchronicities leads us forward. At some level we feel almost compelled to move ahead when the light of an EE shines us on.

To review: It is those meaningful outer events which connect with our inner awareness of thoughts and feelings within an instant of Aha! (regardless of the time span between the event and the awareness) that mark synchronicity. Synchronicities tell us that we are in the flow. It is when we are in the flow that remarkable events and experiences, remarkable things, happen. It is paradoxically, also, when synchronicities happen and we find ourselves in the flow.

So by now you may be asking, "How do I get in the flow? How do I cause a synchronicity to happen?"

Actually, I have learned I can't *cause* a synchronicity. This is because, by definition, synchronicities are acausal. They are not caused by anything we know. They are surprises. They are the recognition, the spark of an Aha! at the very moment an outer event and an inner awareness merge to cause us to remark, "Wow! What an amazing coincidence!" Yet, we can find ways to enter into the flow and then often they mark milestones. By definition it is the surprise or serendipity that gives meaning to the coincidental happening. Actually, for the most part we are stunned into wonder, awe or laughter when they *occur out of nowhere*. This is the same largely for most EEs—they are not produced at will.

The key to note at this juncture is this: When we feel we have some control over our experience, it will not *move* us *as much as had it happened spontaneously*.

Yet, think how you would feel if *all of a sudden, without warning* you see swirls of colors dancing on top of the head of a man when you are talking with him. This happened to me when I was talking with Robert "Bob" Monroe, founder of the Monroe Institute in Virginia. Bob was an older man and the author of books about his out-of-body experiences.[6] While I was sitting with Bob over breakfast, I suddenly saw these brilliant, swirling colors cascading around his head! This was the very first time, in the mid-1980s, when I saw a crown chakra aura. This experience was spontaneous, not expected in any way. It was a moving experience.

So how do we get into the flow, to get into spontaneous synchronicities, spontaneous EEs? Remember to soften and widen your focus (that paradox again!) on what you are experiencing and the events around you. By doing this, you are telling your mind to "pay attention" –something may be perceived that isn't in "normal" view. You have in some way allowed yourself more latitude. You have allowed yourself to venture outward and inward. You are giving yourself a signal that you are doing something different and not the status quo.

Practice softening your eyes, as your eyes are probably your strongest sense. You may find you can "soften and focus" your other senses, too! Because I have worn contact lenses or glasses

---

[6] (1992) Monroe, Robert, *Journeys Out of the Body.* Dolphin Doubleday Publishing, Garden City, NY.

since five years old, I have developed an exquisite sense of touch. Touch is almost a paranormal sense for me; it is so acute. If you read stories or talk with someone who has a sensing disability, you may find he or she has compensated with another sense to the point the individual is "stronger" than "average" with that compensatory sense. For strongly intuitive people, this can go even beyond the known five senses, where intuition, a so-called sixth sense, becomes a daily tool.

So, what are some ways you can develop your ability to be in the flow? I have put together a short list of some ideas to get you going . . .

- Remember to defocus your senses while focusing your attention on something;
- Begin keeping a daily journal to "loosen your thoughts." You may find you start automatically writing intuitions from your subconscious mind;
- Take some moments to simply watch and be with Nature's beauty. Reflect on her life cycles. Write about it;
- Recall just one moving EE of your past and write about it. Consider why it is important to you while you write;
- Be Mindful—pay attention to what is going on at that exact moment you are paying attention. Be in the moment;
- Reframe or look back on a painful life event and see it in a new light in hindsight. Write about your shift of thinking;

- Begin to remember your dreams. Keep a journal at your bedside to record key words from a dream so you don't forget the dream later, when working with it;

- Go to a seminar, museum, zoo or retreat. Go somewhere different than the status quo to learn/sense/enjoy something new;

- Challenge yourself to take up a creative hobby such as music, writing, painting, drawing, cooking, gardening or pottery. Have fun with it;

- When something/someone fleetingly crosses your mind, pay attention, and if you can, act on it, such as calling that friend or writing about it;

- Pay attention to your hunches. Practice, practice, practice. Write about them;

- Write a gratitude list of all the things and people in your life for which you are grateful. You may find you become filled with a feeling of Grace;

- Give yourself a simple challenge every day such as cooking a new dish, wearing something sexy for your significant other, writing an intuitive poem, planting a colorful flower, hiking in the country, practicing seeing auras, and so on. Get out of your comfort zone;

- Try to use your computer mouse with your non-dominant hand and write at the same time with your dominant hand. Now try it the other way;

- Recall a particularly happy time—relive it. Write about it;
- Call or contact an old friend for no reason at all just to say "Hi, how're you doing?"
- Be flexible. If what you want is not available, look into a safe alternative. You may discover you have a winner!

These are some examples we can use to get out of our daily routine of thinking and being. The goal of the above points is to find new ways to get into the flow where you are then more open to EEs, including synchronicities.

In the next chapter I will share more about exceptional experiences and exceptional human experiences, and how they can and do change our lives.

Chapter 3
Potential EEs/EHEs—Your Challenge

As we learned in Chapter 1, we tend to tune out many experiences, mainly because they are common and not really notable to us. We humans have a remarkable ability to selectively attend to only a few important things at a time; otherwise, we would be overloaded with input to our brains and overwhelmed emotionally. Then there are the times we encounter an event which conveys an inner awareness--the power to give pause. We ask, "What just happened?" or "What is going on here?" It is at those times when the outer event and the inner awareness merge to give us an exceptional experience (EE). The EE has captured our attention *and* we are paying attention.

In Chapter 2, we spent some time discovering new ways to expand our awareness in order to have a broader, deeper and higher sense of our surroundings. Part of this expanded awareness, I suggested, leads to *being in the flow.* Once our senses have expanded, even for a few minutes during those exercises, we may find an unusual event occurs or even more awareness develops: For examples, maybe we receive a phone call about a new job location that changes the direction of our life. Or, spontaneously we see auras. Or, a dream comes true. Any one of over 400 different types of EEs can happen to us, or better said, *we happen to it.* An EE arrests us—it is something out of the norm for us. The EE has grabbed our attention and we are thrown for a loop.

On the other hand, we may forget, disregard, or discount the EE. It then fades into memory either in fear or by deliberate action such as shifting awareness to something else. A good exercise is to look again at an EE from an earlier time. Pick one exceptional experience and evaluate whether it is important today and why you left it to "die on the vine" back then. Were you afraid to look into it more? Were you just too busy to deal with it? Or, did you feel it was not important enough? I have dismissed or forgotten many EEs over my lifetime. Yet, for the ones that endure, they are like the brilliant colors against a gray or neutral life tapestry which almost command me to stop, think, process and do *more* with them.

Once I am in the flow, EEs occur often. I am simply happy to go along, as life events seem to be going my way during that particular time. It is in those periods I often do not take the time to evaluate my EEs, such as synchronicities that "tell" me I am in the right place at the right time for the right reason. I am awed, certainly, but am almost used to them being a natural part of my life. I am convinced today that exceptional experiences are a natural part of all of our lives: Remember, we are exceptional human beings having exceptional experiences. We simply need to pause, evaluate, ask questions about what they are telling us about the greater world/Universe at large, and activate them further this way. We have choices.

When we activate EEs, we transform or activate something deep within, we transcend everyday reality. Another word for this type of activation is to "potentiate." In this way, we are discovering the deeper and wider potential of an EE and literally *its power to transform* us. We pay greater attention to the EE. It has moved us in some way we may be able to express, or we may not be able to express. Yet, by taking the EE within our awareness, within ourselves, we are *humanizing* the experience and it becomes an exceptional human experience. *It shifts us inside* and we become an exceptional human experiencer, an EHEer.

It is very important that you understand the difference between the EE and the EHE. At first, I wrote many of my accounts of EEs, thinking they were EHEs. Rhea, would remind me of the difference: Had the EEs *moved me* to further examination? Had I potentiated them? Did the EEs shift my way of thinking or sensing the world and my place in it? For me, that process of moving the EEs forward to potentiate them happened, in some cases, years later, when I was writing about them for my EHE autobiography and my two memoir books.

Here is another key: When you can check off from the list (in the Appendix) many types of EEs that have occurred over your life, you may find that only a few have been powerful, life-changing, paradigm-shifting events that caused you to re-evaluate the world/Universe and your place in it. That is the true meaning of an EHE— we have potentiated it and are further along in our life purpose. We are realizing our potential. We are no longer the same persons because we have transformed the EE into an EHE. It is an active process within us when we humanize our experience. The potentiated experience brings us closer to our authentic self—the person we truly are.

Remember the earlier discussion on double vision? Double vision is when we have a shift in how we envision or sense the world and our place in it. Remember, for our purposes this shift is called an inner paradigm shift. In a paper I wrote for the journal *EHE* entitled "Exceptional Human Experience: Rethinking Anomalies and Shifting Paradigms," I stated, "Over time, or additional EEs/EHEs, or with a tremendous burst of insight, a subjective threshold is crossed. The EEer's lifeview and whole worldview changes, and a new perspective (i.e., double vision) is forged. Fresh transpersonal connections with a new vision of self and the world become established." [7]Double vision is important to understand, as it truly sets up a new way of being in the world. We may see, hear, taste, smell or touch in new ways—we literally experience the world, and all that is in it, with a new set of glasses.

For example, it was not until I had a vision of a huge, white "jumbo jet" with the markings of "VASA or LASA" on its side exploding in the air, that I believed it is possible to have precognitive awareness. I saw in a vision the NASA Space

---

[7] Brown, S.V. 1997a Exceptional Human Experience: Rethinking Anomalies and Shifting Paradigms: An Introduction and background paper, In R.A. White (Ed), Exceptional Human Experience: Background Papers II, (pp.21-26). New Bern, NC EHE Network.

Shuttle Orbiter *Challenger* explosion the day before it happened. (When we perceive something before it happens, it is called *precognition*.) When I watched the explosion on TV, as did a million other people on January 28, 1986, I was stunned! In my vision, I thought it was a midair plane explosion, but here was the Challenger disaster and I saw it happen as it happened, remembering my vision from the day before. I had even told a couple of friends about my vision before it happened, because it was so shocking to me.

My focus at the time of the vision was this big plane with letters on it blasting apart. I tried to gather all the descriptive information I could. I knew it was precognitive—it had that "feel" to me. Because the vision was over in a few milliseconds, I felt I had to capture it.

When the actual Challenger disaster occurred, I was having an early lunch with a girlfriend at a restaurant and watching TV. At the moment I saw the explosion, I felt stunned and terribly troubled. I really understood and believed deeply for the first time that this precognitive stuff was real. And, at the same time, I was so distressed for the caring families of the astronauts and our country.

We all had lost so much that day. We lost some of our hope in the NASA program—some of our national pride was diminished. The television kept showing the scene of the explosion in the air over and over for days. More and more people around the world tuned in to this catastrophe. I felt the worldwide sadness for such a loss of promising lives as a huge weight. Could I have done something anonymously? Who could I tell about that vision? In the end, I realized I did not have enough information to have helped prevent such a disaster.

Because of this experience, I no longer wanted to have these types of visions and dreams. They were distressing. Something within me shifted. The older way I had of seeing the world through mainly mainstream, scientific eyes, which ignored or discounted precognitive visions and dreams, had changed. My personal lifeview, shifted at the moment I saw the explosion on TV— I could no longer go back to discounting my experiences. In essence, I had opened my mind. Because of this shift within, I had become an EHEer. But what a painful initiation! Over a few more of these painful precognitions in the mid-1980s I learned to tune them out. I no longer wanted to have them, unless they were positive or I could help some way.

Do you see now some of the differences between an EE and EHE; an EEer and EHEer? Double vision is a result or "aftereffect" of your EE to EHE transition. I will speak more to the EHE transformative process later in Chapters 4 and 5.

One more note about having EEs and EHEs: They are often difficult to articulate. I suggest you keep a personal, dated journal of your daily experiences, including EEs and any insights you gain from them. As you write, you may shift your perspective on your EEs. You may find they "become" EHEs during your writing process. Another key is when I became used to my experiences or I simply had more, I was able to talk about them easily with other people. I found the words I needed to express my EEs and EHEs. See if that is the case with you, too. With EEs and EHEs we almost have to learn a new vocabulary and practice a new way of speaking! I will say more on writing your EE/EHE accounts and EHE autobiography later.

In Rhea's and my work with the Exceptional Human Experience Network (EHEN), we identified five classes of EEs/EHEs. All five and the representative types of experiences have the ability to move us; to shake us up and give us a new worldview rich with double vision. Indeed, no particular experience is "better" or "more powerful" than another, as it really depends on the experiencers themselves. Let's face it; some experiences just have a way of striking us. We would then be more apt to actualize them. Yet for all intents and purposes, we will treat all classes and types of EEs/EHEs as *potentially* life-changing and paradigm-shifting.

The five classes of EEs/ EHEs with some examples are:

1. **Psychical**: telepathy, precognitive vision/dream, out-of-body experience;
2. **Mystical**: ecstatic bliss, cosmic consciousness, conversion experience;
3. **Death-related**: near-death experience, past life recall, haunting;
4. **Encounter**: shrine/power place, UFO, ancestor;

5. **Enhanced normal**: sports zone, déjà vu, nostalgia.

Now, please go to "Appendix II—List of Potential EEs/EHEs." There you will find over 400 types of exceptional experiences/exceptional human experiences. The list is 23 pages long—there are so many types of experiences! They are in alphabetical order. You may find, as I did, many of the names unfamiliar—the words may seem to come from a foreign language. Don't worry! Rhea was quite the researcher and librarian by nature, and she spent decades reviewing books and articles to do this compilation. You may want to go back to it time and time again as you continue to explore your own experiences and progress.

Take your time with the list and check off the ones that fit your own life. Now count them and get a total. Also, do you see patterns of the five Classes or clusters of types of experiences? To be sure, you may need to use a dictionary because Rhea used a wide range of experiences and had many names for some of them. She could see the subtleties and nuances. Rhea would be inclusive, rather than exclusive, trying to make sure we all would be able to locate exactly our own experiences we've had.

So, were you surprised to learn that you may have had more experiences than you originally thought? When Rhea was developing this List of Potential EEs/ EHEs in the mid-1990s, she gave it to me to review and add on any I thought might be additions. I remember I was astounded at first to see such a list—never before had I felt so validated! When I saw all those experiences she had compiled, and checked off about one-third of them, I felt like I was having another EE!

Now that you have discovered (or rediscovered) some experiences you may not have considered before, write some down in your personal journal and work them over in your mind. Try to see where they lead you as you open to a greater awareness. When you are doing this exercise, please do not consider yourself "crazy" or "an oddball" because you have had some of these experiences. The way to think about them during this time is whether they have moved you to a new way of perceiving the world/Universe.

Rhea and I would say to folks: "Did the experience change your life in some way?" "*Did it move you?*"

Certainly some of the EEs moved me off my center, out of my comfort zone since early childhood. Yet, I had to learn to *ask for help when I was overwhelmed by the stimulation* that came with them. There were times when everything seemed to be rushing into my mind at once or I experienced a rapid sequence of particularly powerful incidents. I needed to learn how to keep my feet on the ground. Thank goodness, these experiences are now called "spiritual emergencies," or "spiritual awakenings," even when they are not particularly religious. The Western world, including traditional psychiatry has been catching on over past few years. One major change is to consider spiritual awakenings as life changing events to pursue and reconcile, rather than as a form of psychopathology and mental illness.

I recall back in the 1980s and 1990s when I was having so many exceptional experiences they seemed to overwhelm me. My doctors agreed. However, in those days I was considered, "abnormal" simply because of my experiences. I have learned since to accept that I am in recovery from my alcohol dependency and mental illness diagnosis. Alcohol was a way of coping with my experiences before I learned that those EEs could be life enhancing. I will speak more on the subject of coping with our experiences and emotional challenges later on.

In summary, you can move outside the box with your thinking and still keep your feet on the ground—for after all, how else do we humans grow? It does not always have to be a painful thing that pushes us beyond our comfort zone. We can have the happiness and the joy that comes from an Aha! realization of transcending an EE— of potentiating an EE into an EHE. The insight we gain may last a lifetime. One such transforming experience was when I was sitting comfortably in my easy chair one evening listening to soft music. I was awaiting a friend's visit and I had "visitors." I will never forget when I closed my eyes and drifted deeply a bit off center, I "saw" several golden beings of light. They were translucent, amorphous beings floating a little above and to the left of me. I "heard" them say, "You are one of us—we are Home." I felt this most incredible sense of *unconditional Love* flow throughout all of me. I *knew* these beings! I *knew* I was to return Home with them someday. I was protected.

I return to this experience whenever I feel lost on my Path. I know I am connected to more than the apparent world I perceive with my five senses. I will never forget that transcending, life-changing EHE!

As you go through your own memories of EEs and EHEs, please focus on where you were then for context and where you are now in hindsight. In brief, see where you have travelled. You may find you have covered a lot of ground along the way after a particularly stunning experience. You may find you no longer are the same person. You may also find you no longer need proof. Because you have internalized your experiences, they are now a part of you. Like a seed that has been planted, they will grow over time and life situations. If we are good stewards of our plants, they will grow and flourish. EHEs can and do grow with us and it is only in hindsight that we discover just how far we have gone because of them.

Over the next two chapters I will introduce you to the EHE Process and then provide more detail about it so you can better locate where you are in your life's Journey. Now that you have perhaps discovered, rediscovered and evaluated some of your own individual EEs/EHEs, we can move forward together with *the flow* of the EHE process. A secret to the EHE Process is that it moves constantly as your life experiences do. Yet, there is no clear boundary between life experiences and exceptional human experiences. Neither do these kinds of experiences flow necessarily "forward." As we shall see in the next chapter, life experiences, exceptional experiences and exceptional human experiences include foresight and hindsight in the process of moving. So, let's move onward again!

Chapter 4
Introducing the EHE Process

Now that you have identified one or more exceptional experiences of your own, what do you think? Why did you select that particular experience(s) over another? Did it grab your attention recently? Or did it occur many years ago and still continues to astonish or even disturb you? Such experiences from the past can indeed have the real power to capture our attention and hold it for years. From Chapter 2, recall that even a simple déjà vu or a meaningful coincidence may give you reason to reflect, or laugh aloud with surprise. Where do you go from here?

I am hoping that you took the time to write in your personal journal or share your experience with a friend to help you better articulate it. It is important to communicate our experiences so they don't hold us hostage in fear or worry, or convey a sense of self-importance.

Our EEs and EHEs are markers and milestones and no one's Journey is any more exceptional than another person's. What *is* different, however, is that we are now at a stage in our lives when we have learned to recognize and apply our EEs/EHEs to our personal growth. This recognition and application of our experiences to *perceiving our life as a Journey* is a wonderful metaphor. Because of our EEs/EHEs, we begin to acknowledge and follow our higher, deeper and broader calling.

As Rhea and I reviewed EHE accounts and autobiographies submitted to the EHE Network for our research collection and publications, patterns came to light. The strongest pattern showed a process that begins immediately after the initial strange or odd EE is recognized. Rhea and I discussed this at length, as it came up time and time again. We saw that there were great similarities across these personal narratives. We then reflected upon our own stories. Together the narratives of the contributors and our own experiences showed us distinctive characteristics of change a person undergoes. We discovered that *change itself* is an exceptional human experience, once it is recognized as life-changing! For example, with the gift of hindsight we realized an originating experience sent us on our way toward our individual callings. This recognition becomes an Aha! *Our change and recognizing our change is an EHE!* When this happens, we call this the Exceptional Human Experience Process—*the EHE Process.*

The EHE Process is a key to the evolution of Self. When we look in hindsight at how we have changed, how we got from there to here, beginning with an EE, we are on our Journey. This is not a unique concept; hundreds of writers of books and articles, numerous seminars and workshops have suggested life is a journey. The difference is that Rhea and I specifically looked at any type of anomalous, out-of-the-ordinary, unusual and stunning exceptional experiences as a starting point of the EHE Process Journey. We cast our net widely to include all types of these experiences, not simply one type, such as near-death experiences or precognitive dreams.

The EEs are transmuted, shifted, into EHEs because we have potentiated them—we have actively questioned them. We are consciously working on them. *At the same time, whether we are aware of it or not, they are working on us.* As a result, they are brought forward into active consciousness and become part of us.

A special note here: The experience may work or fester or play with us in background memory for some time, even years if we "forget it" or otherwise let it go. Similar to the tip-of–the tongue phenomenon where you can't quite recall something, but it is "in there," so too is the background processing of an experience that has been forgotten or ignored. It may be waiting behind the scenes, silently biding its time until one day you suddenly remember it when taking a shower or lying awake in reverie. All of a sudden your memory is sparked.

What I really want to stress is that the *activation* of the EE to change it into an EHE—the potentiating process—is a conscious one. You must bring the experience forward in your mind and work with it in order to potentiate it. You must activate it to potentiate it.

Rhea and I hypothesized that our EEs and EHEs have a cumulative effect. Once you begin to sense the process at work, that is, shifting from an EE to an EHE and beyond, your life will begin to change. Life-potentiating experiences begin to happen. With hindsight, this is a major finding of EHEers—life has changed. As discussed in Chapter 2, you are *now aware* of being in the flow. As best you can, stay with the flow and be open to recognize your marker milestones; recognize your synchronicities and exceptional experiences along the way.

Once you begin to change your thinking, feeling and being—that is, realize some of your higher human potential—the door is opened for you to realize "the More" of who you are. The "goal" of the EHE Process is for us to realize our greatest human potential. And, the process never ends—it just gets better as we learn more about ourselves and the interconnectedness of all things. It is an amazing, life-affirming process!

Probably the most important observation Rhea and I made in studying the accounts was detecting the EHE Process. We identified five stages. We learned that expectations, culture, setting, and personal interactions have as much to do with an overall response to a provocative event as do the contributing factors of the event itself. In other words, you may respond to a ghost differently than someone whose culture or family accepts ghosts as a comforting presence from an ancestor. Or, you may have had a stunning near-death experience where you felt unconditional love and were asked by a being of light whether you wanted to go on. If you are an atheist or agnostic, how would you respond? Would that shift your worldview? Or would you dismiss it?

The EHE Process is dynamic. Once the EE occurs, and it is of sufficient strength or notability to rock you, you are on your way. Let's go into the five stages and discuss each of them separately:

1.   Initiatory Experience/ Event
Primary Search: Meaning of the EE.

The EE crosses some personal threshold of "normal" events. It disrupts the status quo and promotes *cognitive dissonance* between the daily and the extraordinary expectations. In psychology, cognitive dissonance is the mental stress or discomfort experienced by an individual who holds two or more contradictory beliefs, ideas, or values. The EE is outside of your everyday worldview or level of expectation; you are confronted with an event you cannot explain or explain away. You may feel uneasy or even distressed. Typical reactions are: Fear of losing your mind, fear of being possessed, overwhelming wonder, laughter, hyperactivity, telling everyone who will listen or telling no one. You search for meaning of the EE along authoritative culturally accepted information resources, such as traditional doctors and counselors, university scientists, or you study authoritative texts. You may return to your childhood religion seeking answers.

2.   The Search for Reconciliation
Primary Search: Meaning of EE in New Context

Authoritative explanations are insufficient to answer Stage 1 questions and resolve your cognitive dissonance. You decide (to make a decision is a forward-moving, potentiating activity) to search for answers outside of the common, traditional resources. This stage is highlighted by searching and discovering new ways of coping, experimentation and exploration. You may be totally consumed to settle the experience back into the "norm." Yet the methods here are different from Stage 1: You visit *non-traditional* practitioners such as holistic doctors, shamans, gurus, psychics, or all-faith churches seeking answers. You're casting a wider net and breaking out of your comfort zone. You may begin a dream journal, listen to "New Age" music, convert to a new religion, take up yoga, or enroll in parapsychology seminars. Sometimes at this stage, experiencers may feel a sense of specialness, and ego inflation. It is also at this stage where the experiencers are most likely to drop out of the mainstream, blatantly try to convert others, and declare him- or herself a "chosen one."

3.   Between Two Worlds
Primary Search: Meaning of Self

Stage 3 can be a relatively sterile, dormant, and even conflicting stage. You have questioned the authorities and found their answers lacking. Discoveries in Stage 2 have revealed a whole new way of perceiving yourself, others, and the world. You now perceive you are part of a greater whole than you were before you had the initiating experience. You are aware of two "worlds" of living and being: your former worldview in which you did not acknowledge or even allow your EE as something "real" before and your newfound worldview where you are open to your experience and the possibility of additional experiences.

Some experiencers may undergo a major identity crisis. No longer able to revert to the old world and still not sure what the new one has in store, experiencers often report they are "outsiders," "lost," or "walking a fine line." Choices in lifestyle, partners, or career may change as you may be indecisive between the worlds.

A remarkable thing about Stage 3 is that you may enter it from either Stage 2 or Stage 4. After all, you may have already had a glimpse of the experiential paradigm (EP) or been catapulted into it by a particularly powerful EHE.

4.   In the Experiential Paradigm
Primary Search: Meaning of Higher Self

At this stage EEs become EHEs. You have integrated your newfound worldview producing a larger, assimilated worldview. You now have double vision. This is when the either/or of Stage 3 becomes the both/and of Stage 4. No longer exclusive, you are inclusive—including all old and new ways of thinking, perceiving, and being. I like to think of double vision as two circles intersecting in the middle to some greater or smaller degree— a Venn diagram. In your personal Venn diagram of double vision, think where your worldviews intersect and where they diverge. What has changed in your perception of the world? Using hindsight, compare where you were then, before your EE, to where you are now. Do you see the difference?

Can you see how far you have moved along your Path since the originating event? This is your search for your higher Self, your higher Purpose. You may want to consider this particular search a spiritual one, although it may not be religious. Each EE transmuted to an EHE adds on to the experiential paradigm. You realize you are constantly growing, evolving toward something that draws you forward. It is a mystical Journey—full of mystery and seemingly fortuitous experiences. We feel we are in a state of Grace. Synchronicities happen. We are in the flow. Mood, overall health, creativity and lifestyle choices are generally positive and balanced. Setbacks are taken in stride and often with a philosophical attitude. With this new vision, you may choose to go back to school, volunteer for a charity or mentor someone.

When a fresh, surprising EHE propels you directly into Stage 4 and back to the more questioning Stage 3, you may think you have lost ground. In actuality, this, too, is part of the process. What we have learned is that the EHE process is reiterative. That is, it goes forward and back, repeating stages as each EE and EHE carries its own strength to place us at the various stages. For example, I might have had a particularly wondrous cosmic experience that thrusts me directly into Stage 4. I did not even go through the questioning and seemingly frantic activities of Stages 1 & 2. Nor did I think I was between two worlds. I simply enjoyed the awesomeness of knowing "the/my truth" that everything and everyone is connected. Sooner or later, however, I would have to come down from my pink cloud and deal in the "real" world—the old world. How do I get my feet back on the ground with this incredible, deep insight I have gained? That is when I go to Stage 3 for the first time; I need to resolve my dissonance and be able to live in both worlds by going forward and back as needed.

5.   A New Way of Being in the World
Primary Search: Meaning of All-Self

With reflection and hindsight, EHEers often report that the originating EE and the subsequent pathway often seemed somehow fated. EHEers feel guided (not controlled) to fulfill their destiny, and thus contribute in their own unique ways their talents and life experience. EHEers at this stage recognize others on their paths and it is the process which unites them; it is the Journey that brings us together.

There is a peaceful assurance that everything is right where it is supposed to be and needs to be—everything is just right. When I am "off" on a certain day, this is when I go back into my cosmic consciousness experiences where I discovered everything is connected and interrelated. It soothes me. I remember deeply.

Yet, we are not saints, just regular folks trying to make a go of Life—a good go.

We are realizing our potential to do More than we did and be More than we were. Sometimes this is as simple as helping an older lady cross the street! I like to think we are planting seeds wherever we go. Because we *know* we are connected to all things, we venerate all things. Nature's cycles and beauty is revered and respected. EHEers feel no need to justify themselves. Our Path has led us to wanting to make a positive difference for our families, communities and the world. In some humble way, our work in any capacity is our life's work.

Highlights to Keep in Mind

- The EHE Process is a series of subjective and objective milestones of human potential for growth, development, and personal and humankind evolution.
- It is reiterative. EHEers may return to any one or all stages. Subsequent iterations are typically generated by a new EE or may be generated by revisiting a particularly powerful EE/EHE.
- The challenge is to bring your focus of attention away from the evidence to prove your EE. Instead, begin to ask questions of your current worldview, its contexts and your philosophy of life.
- The EEer/EHEer's counselors, colleagues, family and friends will be the most concerned about behaviors, actions, and changes you make in the first three stages.
- The archetypal Journey is often portrayed in mythology, folklore, fairytales, parables, divination systems, literature, storytelling and other forms of art.

In Chapter 5 you will be given a Traveler's Map to help you better determine where you are in the Process. My goal in the next chapter is to help you see just how far you have come along in your own evolution toward discovering your calling and a new way of being in the world.

Chapter 5
The EHE Process—A Traveler's Map

In this chapter, I present a more detailed description of the five stages of the EHE Process. I call it a Traveler's Map. I share, in detail, a total of twelve milestone markers for each stage of the map. You are already familiar with the first three markers for each stage in the last chapter, including: Definition, Examples and Primary Search. Here, I will be expanding and detailing more about these three and adding nine others. Together we are building on what we already know. As a result, we are building momentum.

The remaining nine markers are: Questions asked; Cognitive dissonance; Depotentiating activities; Results of depotentiation; Potentiating activities; Results of potentiation; Challenges; Critical juncture; and, Crossroads to the next stage.

"Depotentiation" is essential to understanding the Process: This term refers to the various ways you may go out of your way to not potentiate or actualize the meaning of the experience. You may dismiss the experience, forget it, or otherwise not want to deal with it. It is the opposite of potentiation.

As you review the five stages by twelve markers for each stage, you will see just where you are in the overall process—where you are on your Journey. You may see familiar marker milestones you may have already discovered and passed, such as, "Am I crazy?" or "Which world is real?" You may also see other marker milestones may be still to come. It is my hope that this map will give you encouragement and lessen any concerns you may have.

In addition to the database of EE/EHE accounts and EHE autobiographies emailed or mailed to Rhea or me, Rhea also collected stories from reading autobiography books and saving some of the experiential accounts she found to her EE/EHE database. We learned in our review that advanced EHEer autobiographical reports were few, when compared to the overall inordinate number of EE/EHE accounts we received. We surmised that the advanced EHEers were simply getting on with the business of Stage 5: A New Way of Being in the World. We hypothesized that those in Stage 5 no longer had the desire to talk or write at length about their experiences or explain to others how an initial EE got them "t/here."

I realized more than twenty years ago that it is important to share the traveler's map, and then let others find their own way. Each Journey is unique. After all, my way is not your way. This map, however, is my way of giving back to you and others who are also wanting to grow within your own calling; wanting to get on with the business of Life. You will see the twelve markers across the five stages are general. The *descriptive milestones* (such as, "You locate a mentor . . . ." or "You are challenged to avoid the common pitfalls of guru worship . . . .") within each of the twelve markers, however, are unique to each stage. This will give you a sense of where you fit most, as you place yourself within the roadmap.

Similarly, in a road trip you are taking from START to FINISH, you note on the city map a street you must cross first, then an Interstate you must get on. The street and the Interstate are both markers: If you have passed them, then you are closer to your destination. The key to this map is to recognize these milestone markers and understand they are suggestions based on our data. Speaking again about your road trip, you could choose to bypass the interstate and go a longer, more leisurely route. Or, you may choose to simply drive and go with the flow, having no particular destination in mind. There are many ways of traveling and each place on the map is as unique as you are.

You have had a very general overview for each of the stages and first three markers in Chapter 4. Now, you are welcome to take in as much or as little detail as you wish with this detailed map. My hope is that you will be better able to locate milestone markers already passed and find those yet to come on your Journey. Maybe you will see where you have depotentiated some of your past experiences. In any event, enjoy your travels!

A Matrix Model
of the EHE Process with Characteristic Map [8]
Stage 1: The Initiating Event/Experience
Definition: Your initial, originating Exceptional Experience (EE) is of sufficient strength or potency to capture your attention and disrupt your equilibrium—your "normal" everyday life activities.

---

[8] The initial publication of this Matrix Model was published in the *International Journal of Parapsychology*, © 2000, Parapsychology Foundation. Vol. 11(1), 69-111.

Your EE may be one of over 400 types reported by experiencers and initiated by one or more of a variety of physical, physiological, psychological, or spiritual (that is, intangible) anomalous events. Recall that EEs are classified as either mystical, psychical, death-related, encounter, or enhanced.

Examples: (Psychical) precognitive dream, telepathy, out-of-body experience; (Mystical) ecstatic bliss, cosmic consciousness, conversion; (Death-related) near-death experience, haunting; past life recall; (Encounter) UFO, ancestor; shrine/power place; (Enhanced) in the sports zone, nostalgia, déjà vu.

Primary search: Meaning of the EE.

Questions asked: What just happened? How can I explain this? Am I crazy? Possessed? Am I losing touch with reality? Who can help me understand?

Cognitive dissonance: Your EE lies outside of your everyday life view or belief structure. The experience temporarily shifts focus away from your usual state of awareness and thinking. Your balance, your status quo, is disrupted.

Depotentiating activities: You may exercise one or several defense mechanisms, such as denial, repression or rationalization so that the experience and its inner conflict may be consciously ignored, lessened, explained or laughed away. You may compartmentalize your life activities in efforts to revert to your pre-experience way of life: the former status quo. Your choices are viewed as either/or; reality is black or white. You may ridicule other experiencers and their experiences with vehemence.

Results of Depotentiation: You shut down to experience.

Potentiating activities: You read authoritative books and papers. You may contact and communicate with relevant mainstream scientific, religious, counseling authorities. You share your EE and fears or excitement with significant others. You may meet and discuss your EEs with other experiencers. You may choose to record your EE and thoughts/feelings about it in a journal. You may develop new interests in TV shows, documentaries, books, research papers, internet to gather information about the EE itself.

Results of Potentiation: You are open to exploring and investigating the EE within the traditional, mainstream worldview. You gather a wide variety of facts.

Challenges: *You need to address the EE directly, investigate it further, and recognize its uniqueness within the overall stream of your everyday life.*

Critical juncture: You realize that your answers may not all be found within the mainstream worldview framework (paradigm). You discover that authorities may not have adequate answers and/or the explanations are not satisfying.

Crossroads to next stage: You have a fresh awareness that there may be alternative approaches for exploration which lie outside traditional ones.

Stage 2: Search for Reconciliation

Definition: You choose to widen your search and seek novel, alternative, and even unconventional perspectives that you previously considered unfounded, even foolish. This stage is highlighted by active, sometimes frantic exploration to discover of new ways of examining and coping with your EE.

Examples: You may look into alternative beliefs such as New Age, Zen Buddhism, Tao, Theosophy, nature-based religions (paganism) or go to different faith-based churches. Or you may try alternative health practices such as acupuncture, regression therapy, massage therapy, homeopathy, chiropractic, meditation or breath-work. You may investigate divination tools such as I Ching, astrology, tarot, and runes or seek out alternative authorities such as gurus, mystics, psychics, channelers.

Primary search: Meaning of the EE in a new context.

Questions asked: How and where do I find truth? Who else has had my experience? What other avenues can explain what happened to me? Am I (my experience) unique or special? Am I just another weirdo?

Cognitive dissonance: You realize that the search itself moves you beyond your previously acceptable worldview framework. You look into novel contexts that can be threatening, peculiar, bizarre, or exotic in your efforts to integrate your EE into a new, revised framework.

Depotentiating activities: You lock immediately into the first ideology, method, or practice that accepts you and your EE, or you become preoccupied with divination tools, ritualistic practices and/or idolizing their practitioners (e.g., guru worship, psychic hotlines).

Results of depotentiation: Your wider search is discontinued. You have converted to a new, narrow framework with its practitioners. Although your focus of authority has shifted to more nontraditional ways, your search and answers continue to lie outside of self.

Potentiating activities: You explore a wide variety of alternatives and assimilate the best of what each has to offer. You maintain a balance of expansion and discrimination in questioning practices, tools, and practitioners rather than taking them at surface value. You may locate a mentor, network, or support group of fellow experiencers who provide an accepting environment without dogma.

Results of potentiation: You have a personal shift of lifeview and the dawning realization there may be many roads to truth.

Challenges: You are challenged to avoid the common pitfalls of guru worship (idolizing another), inflation (idolizing self) and to stay balanced with ongoing shifts of mood, activities and focus. Watch having a "know-it-all" attitude. "Spiritual bypass," that is, a type of emotional numbing, is also fairly common. With spiritual bypass we may dismiss others' concerns for our well-being. In a sense we are telling them they do not understand because we know more now than they do.

Critical Juncture: You discover that all roads may have some truth. You have learned to differentiate the wheat from the chaff—the helpful from the confusing.

Crossroads to next stage: You realize that your EE served as a catalyst into other levels of personal discovery; that exploration of alternative perspectives is enlightening, meaningful, and may generate additional EEs. You desire additional EEs to investigate.

Stage 3: Between Two Worlds

Definition: Your intense search activity of the past stage(s) is muted or put on hold as you take time out to assimilate, digest, and integrate your findings into a new lifeview and sense of self. You endeavor to get back to the tasks of everyday life. You see it as a relatively lengthy sterile, dormant period as you waver between the old perspective and cannot totally embrace the new.

Examples: You may find you feel like an outsider—a stranger in a strange land. You may sense you are walking a fine line, crossing the river or stuck on the edge of the shore. Your feelings are sometimes expressed as "the dark night of the soul," or a return to the underworld (inner world).

Primary search: Meaning of experiencer-self.

Questions asked: Which world is real? Where do I fit in? What was that experience all about anyway in the grand scheme of things (life, reality)?

Cognitive dissonance: You find that neither the old restrictive view nor the new one is satisfactory, yet you may feel you must choose one or the other and often switch between them.

Depotentiating activities: You may minimize and try to dismiss your previous EE(s) and prior search activity. This could include any insights, discoveries and meaning you might have found. Rather than face the cognitive dissonance, you may categorize your experience(s) and quest as an aberration. You may reclassify it as nonsense and lump all anomalous experiences as total garbage. You may return to the everyday world with a particular vengeance to make up for perceived lost time.

Results of depotentiation: You and your search are side-railed for months, years or even a lifetime. Long-term cognitive dissonance festers, and chronic unease, use of defense mechanisms, such as denial or rationalization, and inertia take their toll on your body, mind and spirit.

Potentiating activities: You accept and value the experience. You begin to feel more comfortable with ambiguity, paradoxes, uncertainty and carrying this comfort level back into your everyday activities, even without firm answers. You embrace additional EEs and the meaningful insights they engender. You are thoughtfully and empathetically sharing experience(s) with others and strive to maintain a balance.

Results of potentiation: Your shift of lifeview incorporates the best of both worlds. You accept and integrate all life experience into a coordinated and authentic representation of self.

Challenges: You need to be aware of the common defensive pitfalls, especially when no new insights or meaning appears forthcoming. Another challenge is to realize that exceptional experiences are typically not delivered upon demand or "willed" into being at convenience. You strive to find a personal comfort zone that includes a renewed sense of self. (At this stage you actually may exhibit any or all classical characteristics inherent in the grieving process: numbness, denial, anger, negotiation, etc., while an old self or ego identity dies and a new one is formulated.)

Critical juncture: You have the insight that the experience(s) served as a vehicle toward a new level of self-awareness and as a gateway to greater self-discovery. You accept, understand, and assimilate all of who you are into an (more) integrated whole personality of Self.

Crossroads to the next stage: You are aware that your whole Self is greater than the fragments of who you thought you were. You realize you do not have to choose either one world or the other, but may assimilate, integrate, "choose" both and you are more authentic, healthier by doing so.

Stage 4: In the Experiential Paradigm

Definition: You discover, envision and *know* the world/Universe as one great, interconnected whole of living consciousness, where artificially constructed boundaries of reality are nothing in the "grand scheme of things—essential truth." Depending on your point of entry to this stage, three possibilities could happen: You may be catapulted into it with no prior EE/EHE contextual anchors; or, discover it more or less spontaneously and have some contextual EE/EHE anchors; or, return into it as a "place" for gathering inspiration, fresh insight and guidance.

Examples: You have a fresh sense of *knowing* that you have "awakened," "leaped into the void," "crossed the river;" and "returned home." Your lifeview encompasses double vision, where either/or exclusions may be resolved with both/and considerations. These new findings may, in turn, spur fresh insights while you potentiate and transform your EEs into EHEs. You may find you are innovative with heightened creativity, have more frequent and/or intense serendipities, synchronicities, with a sense of "good-luck" which may lead you to novel creations, discoveries and inventions.

Primary search: Meaning of higher Self.

Questions asked: Where do I go from here? Who else envisions the world as I do? How will I recognize others like me? What are our possibilities? How do we manifest and share them?

Cognitive dissonance: The search that has brought you to a new world pregnant with meaning, metaphor, discovery and vision is not easily conveyed to those left in the old world.

Depotentiating activities: You may be reluctant to explore and/or entertain new lifestyle, pursuits, and professional options that seem to widen the gap between you and those "left behind." You may still cling to old-world emotional attachments. You may endeavor to awaken significant others before their time.

Results of depotentiation: You lock into a routine that allows for a larger world view, but does not investigate options further. You may still be emotionally attached to specific people, values, and things. You may feel the aftereffects of deep sadness and loss of the way your life used to be. ***Potentiating activities***: You recognize, accept, assimilate, and integrate additional experiences into your new lifeview according to your inner criteria for meaningfulness rather than tacit acceptance of consensual views. You recognize other EHEers and the mutuality of a shared path. You more easily shift personal preferences, actions, and social styles as circumstances warrant. You begin to recognize and follow a "calling."

Results of Potentiation: You realize that you have a unique contribution to make—a purpose to fulfill—where you are an integral, dynamic part of the whole, the Universe. You see additional EEs to EHEs as sign posts; your directional compasses of life.

Challenges: You are challenged to discover your purpose and align with those actions, people, and circumstances that fulfill it. Your EHE reminds you to have compassion and love for self and others for the essential "who" that we are. Another challenge includes having the courage to let go of outworn attachments, including belief-structures and any residual reoccurring patterns that no longer serve your evolving self.

Critical juncture: You realize that your purpose/way is integral to a larger purpose/way and that any and all actions, thoughts, emotions and desires are seamlessly interconnected. You understand that perceptions are largely based on personal and cultural worldviews, and that thinking boundaries (for example, cause-effect; time-place) are convenient constructions for our human communication.

Crossroads to next stage: You have an inner awareness that we (the collective All) are dynamic, evolving co-creators of Universe as Universe dynamically evolves and is being defined and co-created by the we (All). You have gained an implicit trust that "all will be as it is," as well as (paradoxically) understanding that "as it is" does not necessarily mean (then yet again it may mean) what it appears to be at any selected perceived moment of time/space.

Stage 5: A New Way of Being in the World

Definition: You forge a personally fulfilling, meaningful path that reflects and sustains your inner calling. You also outwardly contribute your personal best to the world-at-large. You see that both (many, multidimensional) worlds are integrated within and without, represented and *known* as one world of an intricately interconnected singularity where you mirror, reflect and align with Universe. You are consciously aware that individual choices—core actions, thoughts, emotions, and desires (intents)—have the power to dynamically shape outcomes (Universe) and endeavor to live through that knowledge responsively and responsibly.

Examples: You bring your transcendental knowledge, your calling, and your unique gifts "back to earth." Some ways of saying this are that you "return from Home to home," "as above so below," "the macrocosm is reflected in the microcosm," "after the return before the return," "I am another yourself;" and "chop wood, carry water." You sense you are serenely whole and evolving.

Primary search: Meaning of Universal Self.

Questions asked: How do I best align myself, my purpose, my calling with Universe? How can I best serve, given my collection of unique talents/abilities/gifts? How can I contribute to the overall evolution of consciousness, including my own?

Cognitive dissonance: Your experiences have given you a transcendent awareness, where you find an abundance of extensions, branches of possibilities, and depth. You feel you must, with some level of calm urgency, choose a path and get on with the program of life.

Depotentiating activities: You may find a reluctance to recognize that even a seemingly connected, purposeful life can still carry doubts, fears, frustrations, and that these, too, can serve as signposts on your Journey. You may require perfection in yourself and others, and get caught up in controlling and formalizing "the goal" rather than recalling that the process leads naturally to "the goal."

Results of depotentiation: You may temporarily encounter setbacks, indecision by reverting to old outworn, yet familiar defenses. You may make personal demands for perfection or desire to will or control outcomes which stall your sense of fulfillment. You may find you are not moving toward your calling and/or have lost your sense of purpose.

Potentiating activities: You acknowledge new EEs and transmute them into EHEs by questioning meaningfulness. You go inside yourself to resolve old remaining issues, including reviving long-term EHEs that may have been "lost in the shuffle." You now take setbacks and doubts in stride and see them as opportunities to evolve further, learn new skills, meet new people and integrate these contributions into your personal calling. You fully recognize, respect and have compassion for our very humanness, fragments and wholes alike.

Results of potentiation: You are living, being, fulfilling, and doing personal projects of transcendence, that is, you have grounded your inner calling into life-worthy projects. You now have the flexibility to shift means, methods, and tools as needed. You are more trusting.

Challenges: You are challenged to not become stuck in a particular method, means, or mode to accomplish your calling. You realize you are serving as a human embodiment of your higher purpose. At times, you may feel the need to flow back into Stage 3 to regenerate your batteries, and assimilate and integrate new information as needed.

Critical juncture: You realize and have the insight that there is no magic bullet or fast-food package called "the Truth," or "the Way to Enlightenment," nor do you yourself singularly embody truth and enlightenment. You are aware that reality is constantly, dynamically being reformulated, destroyed and re-created. Potentiating EEs into EHEs has more or less become second nature to you.

Crossroads into next stage: You are aware that your dynamically aligning, harmonizing and purposeful Self resonates throughout the universal village—the Universe. You have learned a new way to navigate and negotiate the staging areas of the EHE Process in any permutation as needed when needed. You have returned home to simply be, live, serve, fulfill and embody the More that you are.

Summary

Were you able to find where you are in the Process? Did the stages' milestone markers help you? Do you see now with hindsight just how far you have gone? Do new EEs add to your Journey's progress or do you start over with each new EE? You may have discovered that Stage 3 is your so-called "staging area," where you needed to stop and think about each new EE, but didn't necessarily have to start the Process all over again from Stage 1. If you have gone into Stages 4 and 5, you may have found Stage 3 is a good place to retreat when you need to. In any event, the EHE Process is an invitation to learn more about You!

I will leave a few of these questions unanswered because you have lived these stages for yourself. One-by-one experiencers from all walks of life and across fields of enterprise have explored the depths of inner space and the heights of outer space, and come back home to tell about it. With the EHE Process we live and embody what we have found to be true for ourselves—our truths, our reality. Each experiencer finds his or her uniquely individual way, yet the stories and the explorer maps are remarkable more similar than different. I, too, have woven myself into the fabric of this map and yet remained true to the experiencers who have generously shared their stories over the years.

In the next chapter, you will read about some fellow experiencers over history who made advances in various fields of endeavor, such as the arts, science and invention. You will see that exceptional experiences can and do change lives, even whole cultural worldviews. They also can be history-making.

Suzanne V. Brown

Chapter 6
EEs/EHEs that Changed the World

Many world-shaking inventions, discoveries, creations and leadership choices have been the direct result of exceptional experience. Meaningful dreams, synchronicities, visions, intuitions, and precognitions are especially notable here. The fact is, world-shifting EEs were singled out from the mainstream flow of everyday experiences by folks who recognized a special allure, meaningfulness, even a numinous feeling. These EEs caught their attention. For whatever reason, these experiencers might have dismissed them—depotentiated them—but they did not.

If you go to any search engine such as, Google, Bing or AOL, and type in a significant invention or scientific discovery, you may be surprised to learn that the breakthrough was the direct result of an offbeat experience. Further, you may find famous inventors, scientists, musicians, writers, researchers, leaders and business people became famous as a result of a particularly powerful EE or EHE. Some people have even thwarted an early death *because* of an exceptional experience!

Remember the difference between an EE and an EHE is whether or not the experience was potentiated and shifted an everyday worldview into a larger window. For the most part, I cannot say either way whether the people outlined in this chapter became EHEers, only that they sent large ripples through the world as they changed or redirected history. The account below depicts one instance:

In 1619, on the night of November 10–11, when René Descartes was just twenty-three years-old, he had three paradigm-shifting dreams. Only a year before, he'd graduated in law from the University of Poitiers.[9] Descartes was a soldier in the Dutch Army. On the night in question, he was staying in a house, awaiting his orders. The dark night was filled with a freezing, wind-driven rain smashing all around the house. Descartes was reading a book on music. In the warm room he nodded off a few times and finally went to sleep. He immediately began to dream. In the first dream, he is fighting to walk erect; he keeps leaning off to the left, tottering, and this is uncomfortable for him. As he is dragging himself along, trying to stand up, he misses greeting a friend. Another man, a stranger, enters the dream. He asks Descartes to bring back something to his [the stranger's] friend. Descartes does not know what he is to bring back, and the stranger disappears. Within the dream Descartes feels very disturbed, unbalanced—still not able to walk upright. He wakes distressed, and prays for protection from bad omens.

In the second dream, Descartes hears a bang and while still in the dream lucidly thinks it is thunder. He is fearful of the sound and jumps awake. All around his room are sparks of light; the roaring fireplace had blazed sparks.

The third and final dream that night revealed the most to him: In it, he saw an

---

[9]   http://www.biography.com/people/ren-descartes-37613#early-life

unfamiliar book that named-ancient poets and recorded some of their thoughts. It was lying on a table. Flipping to a page, he chanced upon the saying, "What path of life shall I pursue?" Then another stranger appeared and recommended a piece of verse, "*Est et non,*" (what is and is not). Descartes awakened immediately and enthusiastically began to write. With these dreams, "he understood the key to the true foundation of all sciences had been revealed to him. He felt the dream was encouraging him to pursue a career as a mathematician and a philosopher."[10] [11] [12]

Immediately afterwards, Descartes wrote that he saw very clearly that all truths, as philosophical sciences, were linked. The famous proposition Descartes wrote in his *Discourse on the Method for Rightly Directing One's Reason and Searching for Truth in the Sciences* (published in 1637) has lived throughout the ages—"I think therefore I am."

It is difficult to see how and why in Descartes's mind those particular dreams and that night of dreaming were so life-changing. He had been trained as a lawyer at the wish of his father, yet became a soldier because of his own

---

[10] https//math.berkeley.edu/~robin/Descartes/

[11] https://marilynkaydennis.wordpress.com/2010/08/25/the-three-dreams-of-rene-descartes/

[12] Hatfield, Gary, "René Descartes", *The Stanford Encyclopedia of Philosophy* (Spring 2015 Edition), Edward N. Zalta (ed.), forthcoming URL = <http://plato.stanford.edu/archives/spr2015/entries/descartes/>

aspiration. He had recently been traveling rather aimlessly throughout Western Europe meeting and talking with people from all walks of life until he went into the army. It was a fearful night of storms; perhaps the crashing sounds on the window panes were enough to spook him. At first he was afraid and then the last dream made him enthusiastic and triumphant. It put in front of him the perennial question, "What path of life shall I pursue?"

I have learned that with many, if not most EEs/EHEs, it comes down to whether the experience was *personally meaningful.* Thus, I may not understand why René Descartes interpreted his dreams the way he did. But I do not need to. His choices shifted the way we see science, geometry, mathematics, and humankind for over five hundred years!

Descartes said in his writings that it was revealed to him a new philosophy—the scientific theory of *dualism.* (In Descartes day, science had not broken off from philosophical thinking. Before Descartes, all scientific thinking was considered "philosophy.") In dualism (that is, two aspects) the human body is considered separate and different from the mind. For Descartes, the physical body functioned in a manner similar to all animals. Yet, with dualism, the mind operated separately in a nonphysical realm, under the influence of the soul.

We in the Western culture shifted from a pervasively ruling, traditional, ecclesiastical (church only) viewpoint before Descartes to a more worldly, logical, secular viewpoint. Descartes led the way of the Scientific Revolution with the rise of science through such notables as

Copernicus, Harvey and Galileo. Descartes is often lauded as the Father of Modern Philosophy. After his night of tumultuous dreaming, he eagerly awakened. He wrote later that *knew* his path that night.[13]

When I reviewed some of the materials cited in this short anecdote, I was struck that Descartes *may have been* a Stage 5 EHEer as a result of potentiating his dreams. The reason I suggest this is, by his own account, his dreams changed him and he forged a new way to be in the world.

Do you see just how a "simple" EE for anyone can become life-changing, even world-changing?

There are other notable experiencers in history who made remarkable shifts in the way we envision our world. Because many of them lived in an earlier age, we know of their experiences mostly from anecdotal stories. I have selected accounts that are widely regarded to be valid, passed down through their biographers, their own books or their speeches.

Take the story of American Elias Howe (1819-1867). Contrary to popular belief, Howe was not the first to conceive of a sewing machine. At least 80 patents preceded his—one sewing machine patent as early as 1790. However, Howe originated significant refinements, including inventing the use of a "lockstitch" design, where the upper and the lower threads would lock to hold a seam or garment together. His design contained

---

[13] Clarke, Desmond (2006). *Descartes: A biography*. Cambridge University Press. pp. 58–59. ISBN 9781139449847.

the three essential features common to most modern sewing machines:

- a needle with the eye at the point,
- a shuttle operating beneath the cloth to form the lock stitch, and
- an automatic feed.

It was thanks to a dream recorded in his mother's family history he came up with the concept of placing the eye of the needle at the point:

He almost beggared himself before he discovered where the eye of the needle of the sewing machine should be located. It is probable that there are very few people who know how it came about. His original idea was to follow the model of the ordinary needle, and have the eye at the heel. It never occurred to him that it should be placed near the point, and he might have failed altogether if he had not dreamed he was building a sewing machine for a savage king in a strange country. Just as in his actual working experience, he was perplexed about the needle's eye. He thought the king gave him twenty-four hours in which to complete the machine and make it sew. If not finished in that time death was to be the punishment. Howe worked and worked, and puzzled, and finally gave it up. Then he thought he was taken out to be executed. He noticed that the warriors carried spears that were pierced near the head. Instantly came the solution of the difficulty, and while the inventor was begging for time, he awoke. It was 4 o'clock in the morning. He jumped out of bed, ran to his workshop, and by 9, a needle with an eye at the point had been rudely modeled. After that it was easy. That is the true story of an important incident in the invention of the sewing machine.[14]

Elias's sewing machine won many international awards. He was also awarded the Légion d'honneur by Napoleon III. He died a multimillionaire.

Before Howe's invention, up unto the late 1800's, factories employed girls, even children, for hand sewing. Every stitch on every piece of was hand stitched—this also included upholstery, shoes, leather and sails. These were horrible working conditions. Some factories worked them twelve hours a day, every day, until they lost their eyesight. As soon as their eyesight began to go, the girls were sent home to live a miserable life. Around the globe, the lockstitch sewing machine released thousands of workers from these harsh, relentless conditions.

In the context of EHE: The automatic sewing machine was hugely world-changing. As his mother wrote, Howe was almost a beggar before his invention—before his dream. His dream experience was moving to him, so much so that he woke up in the middle of the night to make sure he wrote it down and tested it. The spears became his design for the needles. He invented the world-changing sewing machine method, wrested his life from death and himself from poverty—spurred into that action by the dream. Whether he had a

---

[14] http://www.world-of-lucid-dreaming.com/10-dreams-that-changed-the-course-of-human-history.html   and http://www.sewalot.com/elias_howe.htm

spiritual awakening of some sort is a question open to speculation, but he certainly potentiated his dream and changed his life and the lives of millions. He lived Stage 5, "A New Way of Being in the World."

Friedrich August Kekule (1829-1896), a German, who after the 1850s was the most prominent chemist in Europe. When a young man he wanted to be an architect, but after he began university, he changed his mind.

By Kekule's own account, he experienced two dramatic dreams that shaped the foundation of organic chemistry. The first dream occurred in late summer of 1855 when he was riding on the upper deck of a horse-drawn, enclosed bus. While he was dozing, he saw a vision of dancing atoms and molecules link to each other. He awakened and immediately began to sketch what he saw.

The second and more famous dream occurred at his residence in Ghent, probably in early 1862. It involved a figure of a snake that had seized its tail in its mouth, making a circle or wheel-shape—the ancient symbol of an ouroboros. Kekule is famous for having clarified the nature of aromatic compounds, based on the benzene molecule. It was a novel proposal and led to the dramatic expansion of the German chemical industry in the last third of the nineteenth century. The year before his death, he was raised to Prussian nobility and took the aristocratic surname "Kekule von Stradonitz." Yet, in contrast to his career success, Kekule's first wife died giving birth to their first child and a later marriage was unhappy.

EVERYBODY'S EXCEPTIONAL, INCLUDING YOU!

This story shows again how EEs can and do change a whole enterprise or industry. Do we need to potentiate our EEs into EHEs in order to have a happier life all around? Kekule's famous career entangled with a more tragedy-riddled personal life story reminds me that life is not always a bed of roses—there can be thorns among those roses. Yet what a difference his experiences had for the world!

As just illustrated, dreams are particularly potent when we are in the middle of solving a problem or have a deep question to answer. Not only do dream EEs have the power to change lives, they can change history. Yet, big or small, when transmuted to EHEs, they get into our core being. Our deeper, inner self changes. I think Descartes felt this—do you think Howe and Kekule felt this, too?

Albert Einstein (1879–1955) seems to have potentiated his EE dream into an EHE by all accounts, as noted in this short, yet famous narrative: When Einstein was still a teenager working in the patent office he had a dream. He dreamed:

I was sledding with my friends at night. I started to slide down the hill but my sled started going faster and faster. I was going so fast that I realized I was approaching the speed of light. I looked up at that point and I saw the stars. They were being refracted into the colors I had never seen before. *I was filled with a sense of awe. I understood in some way that I was looking at the most important meaning in my life.* Much later he reflected, looking back: I *knew I had to understand that dream,* he said, *and you could say, and I would say, that my entire scientific career has been a meditation on that dream."*[15]

Young Einstein dreamed his theory of the speed of light that night. His theory would change the history of humankind in science, technology, and industry. It seems he potentiated this dream into an EHE on the spot, as he said he "understood . . . the most important meaning in my life," rather than, "later I understood." He also wrote he was "filled with a sense of awe." Because Einstein shared that the dream was "the most important meaning in my life," we see an important ingredient for an EHE: Meaning, meaningful and meaningfulness are key words. "Awe" and "meaning" can be signals of a powerful leap directly into Stage 4, into the Experiential Paradigm. In essence, that particular dream was numinous, mystical: it rocketed Einstein into a new dimension of perceiving and being in the world (Stage 5). His statement later in life shows he felt it led to his calling—the EHE never let him go. This is brilliant example of someone whose whole life (and the worldview) changed because he attended to his initial experience, felt the awe and meaning, potentiated it to an EHE, and followed his calling, his Journey.

There are many short, anecdotal accounts of people made famous only because of their EE/EHEs that changed the world in some way. Below is a list of a few:

---

[15]   Source: www. worlddreambank.org. All italics mine

Dr. James Watson (1928-   ), dreamed in 1953 of two intertwined serpents with their heads at opposite ends. He interpreted this dream into his double helix model for DNA. (Some accounts state that Watson dreamed of two intertwining spiral staircases, however his alma mater, Indiana University, states he dreamed of serpents.)

Carl G. Jung (1875-1961) was a native of Switzerland and dreamed often. He suffered a broken foot followed by a heart attack in 1944. During that illness he had a near-death experience (NDE) that absolutely shifted the way he envisioned the world and his place in it. He wrote a several-page account in his autobiography, *Memories, Dreams, Reflections*.[16] Very briefly, he found himself floating high in outer space and had an extensive view of the Earth. From his vantage point he could see the Himalayas, the Indian Ocean and even a black stone the size of his house floating by! Jung spotted an entrance into the stone's antechamber and he began to climb the stairs into the stone building. Jung wrote:

As I approached the steps leading up to the entrance into the rock, a strange thing happened: I had the feeling that everything was being sloughed away; everything I aimed at or wished for or thought, the whole phantasmagoria of earthly existence, fell away or was stripped from me—an extremely painful process. Nevertheless, something remained; it was if as now I carried along with me everything I have ever experienced

---

[16]   Jung, C. G., *Memories, Dreams, Reflections*; recorded and edited by Aniela Jaffe, 1961, Random House, pp. 289-298.

or done, everything that had happened around me. I might also say it was me, and I was it. . . . . I felt with great certainty: this is what I am, "I am this bundle of what I am and what has been accomplished."

Jung went on to describe that there was nothing else he wanted or desired. He did, however, have many questions left unanswered as he approached the temple-rock. He said he expected answers within the rock from people who had known him in life. He wanted to learn from them simply where he and his works fit into history. Just as he was getting close to his answers, an image of his doctor floated up from Europe. Jung was amazed that the doctor was in his "primal form," that is, he was surrounded by golden wreath or chain. The doctor told Jung in his NDE that he must return to Earth as there was a protest when Jung had gone away. Dr. H. said that Jung had no right to leave this Earth and must return. Then the whole vision disappeared, leaving Jung greatly disappointed because he was not able to get his questions answered, or to enter the temple and join the people in whose company he belonged.

It took Jung about three weeks to begin to eat and want to live again. He considered living on Earth, in everyday reality, the "box system," where "the three-dimensional world had been artificially built up, in which each person sat by himself in a little box." However, after a few weeks he began to experience extreme bliss in the nights for about an hour: "It was as if I were in ecstasy. I felt as though I were floating in space, as though I was safe in the womb of the universe . . . the highest possible feeling of happiness. 'This is eternal bliss, I thought,' This cannot be described; it is far too wonderful!'" Everything around him felt enchanted; night after night he "floated in a state of purest bliss. He said, "It is impossible to convey the beauty and intensity of emotion during those visions [during the NDE and nightly]. They were the most tremendous things I have ever experienced. In the chapter "Visions," Jung recounts more visions as well as his nightly ventures into "eternal" bliss (during those three weeks).

How did this incredible and well-documented experience change Jung and the world? Jung writes, "After the illness a fruitful period of work began for me. A good many of my principle works were written only then. The insight I had had, or the vision of the end of all things, gave me the courage to undertake new formulations."

C.G. Jung is most famous today for his many works on consciousness in all its forms. Some of the works you may be familiar with in a variety of settings, such as personality scales and definitions often used in business; for example, extravert-introvert, thinking-feeling, sensing-intuition, and perceptive-judging. Or did you know he conducted astrology research and was a correspondent with J. B. Rhine, the father of research parapsychology? As I have stated earlier in *Everybody's Exceptional, Including You!* Jung is the one who coined the word and defined "synchronicity" as the acausal connecting principle. In his book's Appendix, "On Synchronicity" (1951) and treatise, "Synchronicity: An Acausal Connecting Principle." (1952) he discusses synchronicity as something besides strict cause-effect, mechanical, outwardly observable interactions.[17]

Jung wrote about how "coincidences," may be connected by meaning:

Meaningful coincidences are thinkable as pure chance. But the more they multiply and the greater and more exact the [connection] is, the more their probability sinks and their inthinkability increases, until they can no longer be regarded as pure chance, but for lack of a causal explanation, have to be thought of as meaningful arrangements. . . .Their 'inexplicability' is not due to the fact that the cause is unknown, but to the fact that a cause is not even thinkable in intellectual terms."[18]

One person strongly influenced by C. G. Jung was Bill Wilson, founder of Alcoholics Anonymous (AA) in the mid-1930s. Bill has a story of his own. He likewise had an EE vision that seems to have transported him directly into a Stage 4 EHE. As he tells it, he was a "hopeless drunk." His wife and his doctor had about given up on him and expected they would have to permanently hospitalize him. Then, in 1934, in the

---

[17] Both works may be located in Jung's Collected Works, Volume 8: The Structure and Dynamics of the Psyche, Bollingen Foundation, trans. R. F. C. Hull, USA.
[18] IBID, p. 518f.

throes of a continuing series of drinking bouts followed by countless unsuccessful efforts to become sober, he had a life-changing vision. He called it: a "tremendous mystical experience, or 'illumination.' It was accompanied by a sense of intense white light, by the sudden gift of faith in the goodness of God, and by a profound conviction I was in his presence."[19] Later, in January 1961 he was to write Jung, "My release from the alcohol obsession was immediate. At once I knew I was a free man. . . .In the wake of my spiritual awakening came a vision of a society of alcoholics, each identifying with and transmitting his experience to the next—chain style."[20] The result of Bill's visions was Alcoholics Anonymous and its many offshoots of 12-step programs. AA has helped millions get sober since Bill and co-founder Dr. Bob Smith got together and helped each other, and others, "chain style" over the years.

On a personal note: The writings of Jung have touched me in so many areas; from my early search for answers with divination tools, to my interest in dreams and their meanings, to my consultant work on personality types with the Myers-Briggs Type Indicator (MMTI), to my interest in symbolism, archetypes and the hero's Journey, to my growing fascination with synchronicity, to my finding AA many years ago to help me become sober. I am indebted to Jung for his humanness and his works, which oddly

---

[19] A.A Grapevine, Inc. *Language of the Heart*, 1988, New York, NY. p.273

[20] IBID p.279

enough, I did not learn much about in my basic psychology education. It always seemed to be a serendipity of sorts that I would find his works *after* I got involved with some of the concepts he had introduced.

Frederick Banting (1891-1941), a Canadian physician was carrying out research on diabetes. He could not figure out how to help his patients. One night he dreamed of a unique research procedure and immediately wrote it down. The approach was so successful, he was able to isolate the hormone insulin, which is secreted in little amounts, or not at all, in diabetics. This discovery of insulin has saved the lives and health of an untold number of diabetics. Banting's humanitarian gift to the world led him to be knighted.

Otto Loewi (1873-1961) discovered acetylcholine because of a dream. He was going through a period of unfruitful research. Then he had a dream he recorded in his autobiography: "The night before Easter Sunday of that year [1920] I woke, turned on the light and jotted down a few notes on a tiny slip of thin paper. Then I fell asleep again. It occurred to me at six o'clock in the morning that during the night I had written down something most important, but I was unable to decipher the scrawl." He tried unsuccessfully to recall the dream or interpret his note. On Sunday night he went to bed and awoke between two and three. This was an unusual time to wake up for him and he *knew* what the nature of his dream was. He immediately went to the lab and put his new idea into action. The result was isolating the neurotransmitter acetylcholine that is used today in medicines and for understanding nervous system responses in humans and animals. In 1936, Loewi won the Nobel Prize for Physiology or Medicine because of following up on his dream.[21]

Sir John Eccles (1903-1997) also won the Nobel Prize in Physiology or Medicine—he won his in 1963. His concepts of synaptic neurotransmitters were also inspired by a dream: "In 1947, I developed an electrical theory of synaptic inhibitory action which conformed with all the available experimental evidence. Incidentally this theory came to me in a dream. On awakening I remembered the near tragic loss of Loewi's dream so I kept myself awake for an hour or so going over every aspect of the dream, and found it fitted all experimental evidence." The details were diagramed and published in *Nature* in 1947. [22] The beauty of Loewi's and Eccles's works lives on today. Their dreams led to producing medicines that help hundreds of thousands of people a year.

Niels Bohr (1885–1962) had been trying to figure out what the structure of the atom was. He tried to model the atom in many different ways, yet nothing seemed to fit. Finally, one evening when he went to sleep, he dreamed he saw the nucleus of the atom, with the electrons spinning around it, just like our solar system with the sun and planets. He woke and immediately knew it was right. "When he woke up, he knew what his answer was. Further testing and experiments proved it to be true, and in 1922 he was awarded the Nobel Prize

---

[21] D. Todman. *Inspiration from dreams in neuroscience research.* The Internet Journal of Neurology. 2007. Vol. 9 (1).
[22] D. Todman. IBID.

in physics as a result. He spoke often about how it was the dream that gave him the answer he searched for." [23]

Other people over the years have had EEs and worked with them, potentiated them to some degree. Mary Shelley's *Frankenstein* was inspired by a dream. The full musical progression in the song "Yesterday" was dreamed by Beatle Paul McCartney. George Frederick Handel conceived the last movement of the stunning *Messiah* in a dream. Robert Louis Stevenson conceived of the idea for *Dr. Jekyll and Mr. Hyde* in a dream. Dmitry Mendeleyev saw the full layout and relationships of the periodic table of chemical elements in a dream.

General George Patton (1885–1945) said he used his dreams and intuitions to set military strategies and "see" enemy plans. Patton claimed outright that his EHEs worked for him. To another officer he said, "I had a dream last night. In my dream it came to me that right now, the whole Nazi Reich is mine for the taking. Think about that . . . , I was nearly sent home in disgrace. Now I have precisely the right instrument, at precisely the right moment of history, in exactly the right place. . . . This too will change very quickly. Like a planet spinning off into the universe. A chance like this won't come again in a thousand years."[24] Patton realizes his dream is at the right time and place; he perceives it as life-changing for himself and world-changing for the Allies. Because he acted on it, and on so many of his intuitions and

---

[23] http://www.lisashea.com/lisabase/dreams/inspirations/bohr.html.
[24] Wikiquote.org/Patton

dreams, we can probably safely say he was an EHEer. He used his EHEs to plot the course of history.

Abraham Lincoln (1809–1865) had a prophetic encounter with his own death. You may have read this story. Three days before he was assassinated by John Wilkes Booth in 1865, Lincoln had this disturbing dream:

About ten days ago, I retired very late. I had been up waiting for important dispatches from the front. I could not have been long in bed when I fell into a slumber, for I was weary. I soon began to dream. There seemed to be a death-like stillness about me. Then I heard subdued sobs, as if a number of people were weeping. I thought I left my bed and wandered downstairs. There the silence was broken by the same pitiful sobbing, but the mourners were invisible. I went from room to room; no living person was in sight, but the same mournful sounds of distress met me as I passed along. I saw light in all the rooms; every object was familiar to me; but where were all the people who were grieving as if their hearts would break? I was puzzled and alarmed. What could be the meaning of all this? Determined to find the cause of a state of things so mysterious and so shocking, I kept on until I arrived at the East Room, which I entered. There I met with a sickening surprise. Before me was a catafalque, on which rested a corpse wrapped in funeral vestments. Around it were stationed soldiers who were acting as guards; and there was a throng of people, gazing mournfully upon the corpse, whose face was covered, others weeping pitifully. "Who is dead in the White House?" I demanded of one of the soldiers, "The President," was his answer; "he was killed by an assassin." Then came a loud burst of grief from the crowd, which woke me from my dream. I slept no more that night; and although it was only a dream, I have been strangely annoyed by it ever since."[25]

Lincoln told a few friends the next morning, including his biographer Ward Hill Lamon. On the day of the assassination, Lincoln told his bodyguard William H. Crook that he had been having dreams of his assassination over the past three nights. Crook warned Lincoln not to go to the theater that night, but Lincoln replied he had promised his wife they would go. Lincoln was shot at Ford's theater that evening and died shortly thereafter.

What would you do if you had such a vivid dream as Lincoln did? Maybe if he had listened to his bodyguard, he could have prevented his assassination that night? Would you consider his dream and/or the warning as being in the flow or would you dismiss it? What are your beliefs on this? Have you given them any thought? Do you think you could change the flow?

One of the biggest benefits to transmuting an EE into an EHE is that we begin to investigate and try to answer these deeper questions for ourselves. In Chapter 2, we discussed being in the flow of the Universe. We learned that when we

---

[25] Quote excerpted from Wikipedia/Lincoln, Abraham.

attune to our EEs and listen to our intuition, sometimes we have a serendipitous occurrence or discovery, or a chance meeting comes our way. On the other hand, we have also learned that when we are just getting started in the EHE Process, it is best not to overreact to every urge that comes along. It is a balancing act that gets easier with more practice.

It is often by hindsight we say, "Whew, that was close!" or "Goodness, was I lucky to have been there at that time!" or "Because that phone call interrupted my plans, I was safe!"

There are many anecdotal stories of people who have thwarted death because something interrupted their plans. For example, stories abound about the missed or cancelled passages for the luxury liner *Titanic.* The *Titanic* sailed on its maiden voyage on April 10, 1912 and sank four days later in the north Atlantic after hitting an iceberg. You may even know of a distant relative who planned to travel on the *Titanic* and at the last minute changed his or her mind for some reason.

In the early twentieth century, the U.S. was growing by leaps and bounds. Commerce between Europe and America was flourishing before the beginning of World War I. In those days, America had produced many famous entrepreneurs who had built industries, patented inventions, and made discoveries. Below are just a few of the more well-known people who, for some meaningful reason, did not board the *Titanic* that fateful day:

J. P. Morgan helped create General Electric and built U.S. Steel. Stories say he was responsible for saving America's banking system during the panic of 1907. He had booked a passage on the *Titanic* and paid a deposit. However, rather than sail, he chose instead to have more relaxation in France.

Henry Class Frick was J.P. Morgan's business associate and a well-known steel baron. He and his wife were also booked on the *Titanic* and were to sail with Morgan. However, Mrs. Frick sprained her ankle; thereby, the Frick's cancelled their plans.

Milton Hershey, founder of the Hershey Company, famous for its chocolates, had plans to sail as well. He had already booked a first-class stateroom. However, business back in America intervened, and instead he and his wife sailed a few days earlier on the German liner *Amerika.*

Gugleimo Marconi, inventor of the wireless telegraph and winner of the Nobel Prize for Physics in 1909, was given a free pass on the *Titanic*. However, when business called, he immediately left on the *Lusitania* three days earlier. Marconi said he preferred working with the stenographer on the *Lusitania*. To make this story even more remarkable is that his wife and baby son were to follow on the *Titanic*. However, Marconi's son contracted a fever, so his wife and son waited until the fever went away and did not sail on the *Titanic*. The third irony is that at least 700 people were saved because of Marconi's telegraph and the frantic SOS's that were dispatched from the ship that tragic night.

Robert Bacon, the ambassador of France, had reservations of the *Titanic* for himself, his wife and his daughter. When the new French ambassador was late to meet Bacon, the family missed boarding and instead went on another ship, the *S.S. France.*

Longtime YMCA official and famous evangelist John Mott was given free passes for himself and a colleague. For his own reasons, he declined and chose to go on a smaller ship, the *S.S. Lapland.* When they reached New York and learned of the tragedy, Mott and his colleague were stunned. They looked at each other and one of them said, "The Good Lord must have more work for us to do."

This statement must have been the feeling of most if not all of the people who narrowly missed such an ill-fated journey. Regardless of your religious inclinations or lack thereof, when these historical figures missed sailing on the *Titanic* for whatever reason, they must have felt fortunate. I wonder if they, like Mott, realized there was more to do on their paths and the "miss" was a shift in their destiny. What do you think? Do you suppose when they felt, thought, or *knew* they had survived death it became an EHE for them? John Mott would go on to win the Nobel Peace Prize thirty-four years later in 1946. I wonder whether he thought of his brush with death when he was accepting that prestigious award. Although it is not mentioned in his acceptance speech, somehow I think he did.

One more thing: There was a book published by Morgan Robertson in 1898 named *Futility, or The Wreck of the Titan.* That book eerily tells of a shipwreck, which, in many respects, is similar to the wreck of the *Titanic*. The

Titan was also a British luxury liner on its maiden voyage in the northern lanes of the Atlantic in April. It, too, claimed to be unsinkable, because its newly engineered watertight compartments. It was within two feet of the same length as the *Titanic*, had the same number of propellers (3), and both ships had a woefully inadequate number of lifeboats (20 on the Titanic and 24 on the Titan) for 2,207 passengers on the *Titanic* and 2,500 on the fictional *Titan*. The speed of impact into the iceberg was also similar—25 knots for the *Titan*; 23 knots for the *Titanic*. In Roberson's book, written fourteen years before the *Titanic* disaster, the *Titan* crashed into an iceberg 460 miles away from Newfoundland. Four-hundred and sixty miles was the exact distance away from Newfoundland where the *Titanic* sunk. The obvious details, the names of the ships, their description and fates are all incredible coincidences! I can only assume at this point that Robertson (or anyone who had read that book after April 1912) would have been moved to astonishment.

Yet, after the *Titanic* disaster, the author, Morgan Robertson, denied he was clairvoyant (that is, able to see at a distance) or had somehow foretold the tragedy. Later, after 1912, he modified some of the book details to cash in on his fame. I was saddened to learn that Robertson died of a drug overdose in his New Jersey hotel room on March 24, 1915, at only fifty-three years old. Do you think he potentiated his EE into an EHE? Or, do you think he denied his EE, denied his psychical experience, and depotentiated it such that he took his life three years after the shipwreck? History doesn't tell me the answers. We are left only to surmise.

In addition, there have been many stories of everyday people having averted death by arriving late. For example, on March 1, 1950, all fifteen choir members living in a small Nebraska town were late to practice at 7:20 p.m. For various reasons they did not show up on time: one had to iron a daughter's dress; one had to finish a math problem; another could not start her car; a member wanted to listen to the end of a radio program; and, yet another could not wake her daughter from a nap on time. These were examples of separate and unconnected reasons for the fifteen choir members to be late to practice that night. It is fortunate for all of them—because at 7:25 p.m. the church building exploded.

Recall, we can't force synchronicities or serendipities—they are noted only usually in hindsight when we are in the flow of our lives. It is not enough to simply say, Wow-wee!, Aha! or, Eureka! about an EE. There is something more going on, I think. I see them as gifts from the Universe we can unwrap and explore. Whether the EE is a dream, a vision, an intuition, or one of over 400 types of potentially life- and world-changing experiences, you can, as Patton said, know you are in the right time at the right place at that moment. If you follow your EE, because you recognize you are in the flow, you will potentiate your experience into an EHE. In hindsight, you will catch the meaningfulness, the meaning of why you had your EE in the first place. It is an awesome *knowing; a mirroring back* when you realize something greater than you is at work. You will then know you are in the flow!

For example, if you are honestly concerned about getting on a plane, then check it out: Is someone ill you need to attend to? Does your car break down on the way to the airport? Were you plans interrupted by work? We all need to practice with our intuition and make sure we don't have a lot of false alarms, thinking we are in trouble when we are not. I cannot tell you how to know, yet I trust you will know when it is time to follow up on an EE. Sometimes it takes a few or several overlapping incidences to jive with your intuition, dream, or other EE.

I hope you had some fun in this chapter learning about people whose lives had changed because of an EE/EHE. In some of these accounts you can clearly see the EE was potentiated, at least enough for the EEer to make a full life transition in his or her calling. You, too, can have a lot of fun, as I did, investigating different people you may appreciate in history and see whether they had a life-changing EE or two which shifted them toward making a difference in the way they and we envision the world.

In the next chapter we will go further into the *More We Are* and look into some of the aftereffects and outcomes of EHEs. I will use some of my stories and stories of others to show just how we come to realize and connect to our higher purpose through the EHE Process.

Chapter 7
The More We Are

I hope you enjoyed reading some of the stories of people who were changed by their experiences. Even with the church group in Nebraska, we can only guess just how fortunate they must have felt when for an assortment of reasons they were tardy to the choir practice that fateful night. There is a sense of gratefulness when we realize we are at the right place and time. A friend of mine the other day said she wonders how lucky she is when she leaves a bit later or earlier for work and then finds out she missed a bad car accident. We contemplated that premise together. Sometimes all it takes is getting all green signals or a couple of long red lights! Nonetheless, sometimes just knowing you made it safely to your destination is sufficient to trigger an EE or EHE.

By now you should be feeling pretty clear about your experiences—how they caught your attention and how far you have traveled along your way. As we have learned, often it's only hindsight that the meaning is revealed. When we capture the *meaning of hindsight*, we add yet another Aha! layer to the mix—add a new EHE. Do you see just how they cluster and grow once you potentiate simply one? It amazes me just how a seemingly small déjà vu has the strength to give wonder. For example, when I was writing my story about the déjà vu I experienced when entering my friend's house, I suddenly realized I had been *floating!* I had to question, what else is going on here? I now wonder, many decades later, whether at eight years old I had an out-of-body experience (OBE). It was only in writing it down for *Everybody's Exceptional, Including You!* I realized I had *floated* into the entry and up the stairs to see the rooms and moving boxes there!

That leads to another point: Our EEs are often tied to a creative experience. In the previous chapter, we learned of several inventions, discoveries and projects that surfaced during the "background processing" of a dream. In some of the stories the EEer/EHEer had been working hard to solve a problem, or questioning how to best design or fit or compose a model or story. As I wrote earlier in this book, the creative process is at times similar to the tip-of-the-tongue phenomenon, where we are not quite sure what the word or phrase is. For example, a word is "almost there, just not able to come up with it; it is at the tip-of-my tongue." Psychologists call this an *incubation* process. Incubation is where something is "inside and developing" but not ready to be born. It is similar to a pregnancy. The concept, word, idea, invention or piece of music is, "up there in my head—I am just not able to produce it at will at this time."

Tip-of-the-tongue demonstrates background creative processing. Our EEs may have happened many years ago, and for whatever reason or trigger they may revisit us later to be explored. When I was writing about my déjà vu, I was rediscovering an old EE/EHE that had more to be investigated. In retrospect, I am not sure I ever really potentiated it into an EHE, but now I am definitely moved by the possibility that I may have been having an OBE type of EE within my déjà vu. It was through hindsight, and the creative action of writing that account, that I caught the fuller meaning of the experience. I now consider it potentiated—a full EHE. It adds to the tapestry mix of other EHEs over my lifetime. I realize I will continue my Journey with a more inclusive step—there is more to the world and me than I previously thought. My worldview has been shifted-to more awareness of others who have had out-of-body travels; it makes me want to read and share. I continue to become the More that I am.

This discussion leads to some other major points: The Gift of Hindsight and Becoming the More we are.

Try this: Select an experience. Review it again and perhaps write it down. Think about the aftereffect or outcome you felt immediately following the experience. Were you wowed? Were you concerned? Were you exhilarated or frightened? Ask yourself to try to catch your feeling, your emotion immediately during and afterward your retrospective of the experience. For example, when I realized in hindsight that I had been floating out-of-my body during my déjà vu, I was surprised and in awe. Those were my feelings—surprise and awe.

Now, sense or write how that aftereffect, that feeling, shifts your thinking, your personal worldview. I thought I had never before had an OBE and was amazed by the experience and the possibility. Then I shifted my my personal way of thinking to incorporate a larger picture of myself. That is, I was also an OBEer. My worldview shifted, too. I now realize I may be able to travel to distant locations when I am dreaming or otherwise in some sort of altered state of being, such as with a déjà vu, or remote viewing, or while simply daydreaming.

As human beings, we like to share our experiences. I know when I had those precognitive dreams/visions of the disasters, it was important for me then to be validated by others that I was okay (Stages 1 and 2)—that the dreams/visions could be real through another form of perception. Thank goodness my friends were caring enough to offer comforting words. My worldview shifted such that I now sense that the world, the Universe, is much more mysterious and beautiful and complex than my earlier impression. I have learned *through my EHEs* some more about the tapestry of life, about the veil between the worlds—the different dimensions of Being. This OBE déjà vu experience discovered recently with incubation and hindsight has added more magnificence to my perception of the Universe than ever before!

As Rhea writes in her article "Exceptional Human Experiences and the More We Are: Exceptional Human Experience and Identity," EHEs "serve as a bridge between an old identity and a potentially new one. . . . So each human seeks personal knowledge of his or her unity with all things, once the unity is glimpsed, all of life is made new . . . the undeniable sense of connection to the More that an EHE provides."[26] Rhea makes

---

[26] http://ehe.org; © 2007 Parapsychology Foundation

the point that our personal knowledge of unity with all things is something we seek. To "seek" is an action word; to "seek unity" may even be an instinct we are born with, such as a genetic, inborn trait—a particularly human instinct. From my perspective, I sense I have a sort of "contract" within this life to be the best I can be: the More I am. I have had this sense of purpose, this feeling of calling, ever since I was about four to five years old and had an EHE that changed my life:

I was skipping with my friend Mae to the neighborhood grocery store about two to three blocks from home. All of a sudden, in mid-skip, I was lost in the middle of a vast thought—"You are You, You are One of Us. We are tracking with you, life where you are. You have been with Us before." After I cleared my mind, I saw Mae still skipping a bit in front of me, and she was clearly okay. I realized the thought was mine alone; I then wondered, whether I was the only sentient or alive being on Earth. It was a profound experience I never forgotten. It changed my life then, and I have wondered about its meaning ever since. And about thirty years later, I had the "Home" experience, with the sense of beings in my living room communicating pretty much the same message—that I was one of them. I also had the immediate feeling of *Home*—that this was where I truly belonged—with them.

As very young children, we are sometimes reminded that we may still have distant memories of another dimension, another "place" where we were before this life. This is a difficult concept to share, mainly because as we grow up into adults, or even teenagers, we "forget" our previous lives or the place we came from. To remember where we were before birth is called a *Bardo* experience. "Forgetting" the time between the worlds, between lifetimes, could be happening because we are socialized into our Western worldview. We do not have any "proof" of life before this life; therefore, it is usually dismissed. The child is therefore taught that such thoughts are "wrong." Rhea writes, "I think as infants, if not children, most humans are in touch with the divine. As the consensus world begins to close in on us and close us off, we begin to forget. We are even taught to forget." [27] The point is that we typically have, as young children, some sense of something greater or More than we are. This sense is usually rationalized out of us by our parents, teachers and other significant adults. Sometime during our lives we have an EE. Exceptional Experiences serve as wake-up calls. Once we have potentiated our EEs into EHEs, we have shifted, we have moved from our old identity that holds on to the consensus worldview to one that remembers the More we are. In other words, we have been transformed deep within. We are "renewed" with a fresh sense of purpose and calling—a reminder of something we *knew* from before as little children. It may not happen with the first or even the hundredth EHE transformation, but each EHE places us on a higher, deeper, wider more meaningful road Homeward in this Journey of Life.

---

[27] IBID

To paraphrase Rhea: Exceptional Human Experiences give us a taste of eternity—they are moments of grace when we are given hints as to what is the More. Exceptional Human Experiences are reminders of our connection to the Universe, to each other and to the "parts" of ourselves. We reconnect in the grandest and in the simplest sense of the word to our-Self, each other and to the More. We recognize then that we are in the flow—we are on our Path.

Dick Richardson (1931-2013), an e-mail friend of many years from England, the UK, had a spontaneous, mystical experience one late winter night at home when babysitting his two young sleeping toddlers and listening to music.[28] Dick was twenty-four years old at the time, played competitive chess and in his early years had worked as a driving instructor and shoe salesman. As he was resting in an easy chair in front of the fireplace, the music seemed to envelop him—he began to see blackness with pinpoints of light far away.

> As this event continued I became aware that I "*knew*" the music. That is to say, I knew it backwards, forwards, inside out, one note at a time or all at once; and I could see it any way I wanted to see it. I could become the melody, which I did; I could become the harmony, which I did. I could be one note or

---

[28] Dick's full EHE autobiography narrative is located at ehe.org website; © 2007 Parapsychology Foundation.

the whole piece of the music. . . .
Whilst this divine dance of music in
unison was going on I became
aware that I was of two natures
somehow enshrined in one. There
came a point whilst I was swimming
in this light and music when I
became aware that I was looking at
myself objectively, and it did not
seem strange at the time. 'Myself'
did not consist of a body but only of
light, but I knew it was me.

As the experience progressed, Dick saw
magnificent colors, some completely unknown. He
became the music and the colors. After an
indeterminable time, he was quite concerned
about his sanity. "It was, however, the first chance
I had to think about what the hell was going on;
one minute I am sitting in the chair minding my
own business and the next minute . . . zap, and
the world has disappeared, or I from it—which is
it? I knew for sure that I wanted out from whatever
I was in but there was nothing I could do about it
at all; for I had no control of anything." It was then
that Dick "heard" a voice: "Do you want to go on?"

Dick would go on in this three-hour-long
experience to a self-proclaimed limbo and
paradise and into a resurrection/rebirth. When he
became cognizant again, he began to write his
story and beautiful, meaningful poetry. His
language is colorful, touching a chord deep inside
all who read it: "It is a divine swoon of the
exultation of the love of being; and being a part of
it all," he writes. Also, "I drifted in a slow orbit

swathed in a love which is ineffable, beyond words and full rational understanding, in a wisdom which is beyond dialogue, in a place of eternal and everlasting perfection." Right before he came out of his experience, he "heard" the voice again, telling him it was time to go and, "'It is all well that you must go now, for something out there is in need and you must now be with it: do not fear, it is all well that you must go now . . . now be with it!'"

Dick never forgot those words: "Something out there is in need and you must now be with it." But it was not until he had a second, stunning experience, twenty years later, that the words became clear to him. On a warm, spring day, Dick and his new, second wife took a picnic to an overlook of the Chew Valley near their home. Dick and his dog had been playing and then he took some time to rest and simply enjoy nature. All of a sudden, Nature herself became profound: the humming and chirping sounds and the busy-ness of life activity surrounding him caught his attention. He fell into another swoon, overwhelmed again with that feeling of *knowing* and unconditional love.

Dick reflects deeply on his experiences and sums up:

It is plain enough that not all human beings on earth undergo such events during this lifetime; and yet they must do so eventually, *for it is the evolution of the incarnate soul itself.* There is no evolution in paradise, but only an extension of it. We were not made *for* paradise (we were made *in it*); but we were made for freedom; in a temporal world—a world which we are given the freedom and power to make by way of our own desires and efforts. How incredible! "Here is the 'stuff,' my love, make with it what you will"!

Dick went on to write his book and poetry, and to communicate with many hundreds of people from all walks of life regarding how their experiences with something More, beyond the day-to-day reality, had moved them or not. He encouraged people to look deeply inside and not take the word, viewpoint or beliefs of another human being as "The Truth." Dick prided himself on being called a "guru buster," as he very much wanted others to find their own way. Using some email correspondences we shared over the years, I will cite Dick again. To the end of his days, he supported others in their Journey and also pointedly questioned them, should they seem to be going off track, especially when taking another dogma or another person's truth as their own without inner investigation. We had many stimulating email conversations over the two decades since I first read his EHE Autobiography. Dick was 74 years-old when he passed away in the early spring of 2013. I sorely miss him and our email conversations.

Not all EEs/EHEs have to be as powerful or mind-blowing. Recall, one of my most moving experiences into the More was my "simple" déjà vu, revisited over half a century later when writing this book! Some of my most incredible EHEs come when I know I am in the flow because of a seemingly simple synchronicity. The main point of learning the *More You Are* is investigating, potentiating, and seeking your own Truth. After all, your experience may be a sleeping giant ready to be born or reborn after years of incubation—silently developing and reconfiguring in your psyche, awaiting your attention again.

Back many years ago, when I was working with corporate business, selling large computer systems, I was with a colleague, driving home from conference one very dark, moonless night. All of a sudden, a huge ball of blue-green light totally filled my windshield, streaking right-to-left, aiming for the countryside some distance away. I expected to hear a crash—it seemed that close—but there was no noise, just an uncanny silence and the disappearing ball of light. My colleague and I remained quiet for a few moments, and then he turned to me and asked, "Did you see that?" I nodded. For the rest of the ride we discussed what we had seen. The next day I received the nickname from my co-workers in friendly jest, "Blue Star." That evening, as I was driving home from work, I saw a bluish light seemingly disappear behind my apartment building. Within the week, a car darted out in front of me in traffic. The vanity plate read: BLUSTAR. Amazing to me! Blue stars were popping up everywhere!

Even today when I see them, I think they are reminders of that original experience, with its synchronicities. Patterns of blue stars have shown up in different ways over the decades—such as, a child's plastic blue star-shaped ring my husband found when I was exactly, at the moment, writing about my blue star experiences for my EHE autobiography. Or, an antique tin can a friend gave me showing a picture of the Blue Star Lines cruise ship, to a tiny package with a picture of a blue star; it read: "BLUE STAR RAZOR BLADES." Many, many blue star symbols have been recognized by me because I notice them now. My selective attention was heightened for them because of my initial, meaningful experience and those early synchronicities.

So it may take a simple, initiating EE to start, yet the EE develops over the years. Once it has captured attention, it is brought forward in our minds. We no longer are incubating the EE in background; we have "activated" it, giving life to it, so to speak, by potentiating it into a lifetime EHE. These are the special EHEs that have taken us from our old identity to our new. Each of us must follow our own blueprint of EHEs as they lead us to the More we are. Potentiated exceptional human experiences are reminders of our divine self—our connection with something More than our day-to-day strivings on earth. As Dick's "voice" said, "Something out there is in need and you must be now with it." Dick interpreted this as his calling. This outlined, to him, his higher purpose and a turning point milestone on his Journey.

What have your exceptional human experiences shared with you? How have they been valuable? Have they changed the way you envision the world and your place in it? Please take some time to ponder and perhaps even write down some thoughts on these questions. You may find that simply attending to these questions may prompt further experiences and shift your worldview.

You may discover in this potentiating-process exercise that you re-member or re-cognize or re-call your connection with the More you are, with your divine self, however you interpret that word, "divine." You may have a new or an additional spiritual awakening into levels or dimensions you never thought possible. Together we are learning that discovering and uncovering our "calling" is an ongoing process that never ends. Together we are sharing this Journey called Life.

In the next chapter, I will give some of Rhea White's story—in particular her near-death experience (NDE), and how it changed her life such that she founded the Exceptional Human Experience Network (EHEN). Seemingly always evolving and creating a new, Rhea is a gift to us all!

Suzanne V. Brown

Chapter 8
Rhea's Near-Death Experience and Its Aftereffects

Rhea Amelia White was, and still is, a beacon of light around the world for hundreds, if not thousands, of people. Professors, researchers, editors, authors, experiencers, students, dear friends and regular folks corresponded daily with her. There was something special about Rhea; when you spoke with her, you knew right away she was wise beyond the pale. I felt that way when I first wrote a letter to her in 1988, asking whether she could recommend any articles on synchronicity. Rhea responded with a few journal articles and some of her own thoughts. I was hooked—here was someone else who had the same passion for "meaningful coincidences" (synchronicities) and uncanny experiences I had! Not long afterward Rhea would become my mentor. She would continue to support and help me learn to validate myself during my early struggles to accept my exceptional experiences until her death on February 24, 2007.

Born May 6, 1931 in Utica, New York, Rhea grew up loving golf and would follow professional golfers around the links with her parents. She "majored in English because it was not difficult and went to Penn State because it had a golf course." In fact, Rhea aspired to become a championship golfer. Then something critical happened. Here is that story in her own words written in the mid-1990s:

[In] my junior year in college I had a near-death experience associated with an automobile accident that changed my life. I devoted my life to trying to understand "where" I was when I found myself seemingly above the earth bathed in a sense of unity and singing peace and incredible aliveness, enveloped in felt meaning while my body lay unconscious on the hood of my car. I thought I had died—and it was wonderful. I had never felt more alive. I was "told" that "nothing that ever lived could possibly die." I felt the "everlasting arms" behind me to the ends of the universe. Then I awakened on the hood of my car, unable to move, and in great pain.

Rhea's near-death experience (NDE) changed her life and her life's direction. No longer having the goal of being a golf pro, Rhea entered Stages 1 and 2 in her early efforts to understand what had happened to her. In the 1950's there were no research studies or books or articles on NDEs that Rhea could find. In actuality, there was little to no information available on any exceptional experience. Except for some haunting accounts and some interest in mediumship, such as studies with the renowned trance-medium Mrs. Garrett of the Parapsychology Foundation (PF) and the sleeping visionary Edgar Cayce of Virginia Beach, VA, there were very little published resource materials available. In fact, some of you older readers may recall that most exceptional experiences were not spoken of for fear of being considered, "crazy." For the most part, only family members or closest friends would share their exceptional experiences with each other and not with anyone else for fear of being ridiculed.

It was against this background of the 1950s to 1970s when Rhea forged ahead to learn, to study, and to pioneer in a field that wasn't yet clearly defined. Although she had been accepted into two liberal theological seminaries after graduating from Penn State, she instead took on a research fellowship with J.B. and Louisa Rhine at Duke University in North Carolina. She worked with them in their parapsychology lab, and honed her skills in research for four years before moving to New York to become a Research and Editorial Associate with the American Society for Psychical Research (ASPR) under the direction of Garner Murphy. She wrote:

After another four years I decided to find an independent means of making my living so I could be as heretical as I dared, so I obtained a Master's in Library Science from Pratt Institute in Brooklyn. I began work as a reference librarian at a busy public library on Long Island (where I was to spend 29 years) and began to compile reference works about parapsychology.

I founded the Parapsychology Source of Information Center and began to publish an abstracting and indexing service, *Parapsychology Abstracts International*. I also became editor of one of the major parapsychology journals, the *Journal of the American Society for Psychical Research*, a position I still hold. In 1984 I was elected president of the international society of professional parapsychologists, the

Parapsychological Association. In 1965 while in graduate library school I won the Hans Peter Luhn Award, New York Chapter of the American Society for Information Science, for an essay on the information needs of psychology. In 1992 the Parapsychological Association honored me with its Outstanding Lifetime Research Award.

In 1990, after nearly 40 years, I realized I wasn't going to live forever on this earth, and if I wanted to understand my near-death experience (at least now I knew what to call it), science was not going to show me, at least not the behaviorist type of science that was privileged by academic parapsychology. In 1990 I decided to go back and study the basic data of parapsychology--the experiences people report. But I soon realized that they could not be viewed properly without considering them along with all the other sorts of non-ordinary and anomalous experiences people have. In a vision I saw the need to study all of them as a single class of experience, which I called "exceptional human experience. I have been pursuing this aim ever since." [29]

Over our years together, Rhea shared more about her near-death experience: It happened as she was en route to a dance at Penn State in her junior year with a friend "who liked to dance." There was a ferocious blizzard that night; her friend asked whether he could take the wheel, as she had driven a long way already and was having difficulty negotiating the road. They switched sides and continued up a long, steep hill. Out of the

---

[29] Website: www.ehe.org. About the EHE Network: Personnel

blinding snow, a heavy truck came over the top of the hill and hit them head on. Her friend was killed instantly. Rhea went through the windshield and landed on the hood.

It took Rhea months to recover. I am sure she was deeply, emotionally traumatized, although she kept most of that to herself. Yet, as you read in her story, the experience catapulted her into a lifelong search for answers. Did you catch how her life path suddenly shifted from her desire to play championship golf to *knowing* she had to understand what had happened during those NDE moments "away"?

Rhea's search led her through a growing maze of philosophies, religions, psychology, psychiatry and literature. She even learned and practiced different forms of meditation in order to try to recapture the experience of when she nearly died. The near-death experience began Rhea's lifelong quest for answers. This quest led her far into the traditional and non-traditional searches of EHE Process Stages 1 and 2, even though she was initially, literally thrown into Stage 4. As Rhea writes in "The Aftereffects of my NDE":

I learned how to be a parapsychologist. I learned the scientific approach that is practiced even more intensely today among the small band of academic parapsychologists. Contrary to popular opinion, parapsychology is the exact opposite of a "new age" or "fringe group" and bends over backwards to be scientific. In my opinion, however, the field is moving further away each year from being able to understand experiences, such as my NDE and other psychic experiences, because of an overemphasis on control in the laboratory and in the field.[30]

Rhea also collected literature of all kinds on parapsychology and the philosophies, sciences and humanities. Remember, there was no real study of *experiential* psychology or consciousness in the mid-to-later twentieth century. In efforts to be seen as "scientific," even psychology was pretty much stuck in the laboratory until recently. Similar to Pavlov's dogs, we psychologists studied cause-effect, "black box" behaviorism that demonstrated how when something happened from the outside (i.e., a stimulus), the animal or human response was predictable. For example, I learned that people reading the word "RED" printed in green or blue ink letters are slower to respond, say "RED," than when the word is written in black ink. In contrast, people are predictably faster to say, "RED" when the word is written in red ink.

Never one to give up, and without any relevant resources directly related to her NDE, Rhea began to build her own reference base. It turned out, advanced library science would be a perfect study for her as she continued to collect an enormous list of resources. When I visited Rhea at her home in New Bern, North Carolina, in the late 1990s, I witnessed her huge garage transformed into a library with rows upon rows of wooden card-catalog cabinets. Within each drawer of these cabinets were hundreds of index cards with

---

[30] White, Rhea A.: Exceptional Human Experience: Background Papers I, EHEN, Dix Hills, NY: 1994, pp 135-137.

reference citations across a wide variety of subjects, Truly, I will never forget that sight—the rows of card catalogs, file cabinets filled with reference documents, and shelves of scholarly books and academic journals.

In the late 1990s, Rhea decided to go all in. She would "practice what I had been preaching by devoting the rest of my life to studying psychical and mystical experiences. As soon as I began looking into them, I began to see connections between different types of experiences." [31]   As Rhea shared with me personally and in her writings, it began to dawn on her that there might be a *continuum* along all types of anomalous, unusual experiences and that researchers studying one group, such as NDEs or ESPs or UFOs, would not necessarily catch this essential fact. Rhea began to look at this paradigm-shifting insight from a variety of angles and invented a global name to cover all experiential groups along this continuum—Exceptional Experiences. Within that shift, Rhea also broadened her scope to include collecting resources and accounts of all kinds, and encouraging experiencers to find *meaning* within them.

At fifty-nine, Rhea began a doctoral program in sociology at SUNY Stony Brook. Then, toward the end of her life she enrolled with the Institute of Transpersonal Psychology (now called Sophia Institute), where she could work directly with encouragement from the faculty on her dissertation regarding Exceptional Human Experience. Rhea and I met again in 1998 to

---

[31] IBID

present at University of Arizona's international consciousness studies' conference, "Tucson III: Toward a Science of Consciousness." We conducted a workshop on "Being in the Zone" and presented the overall theory of EHE and the EHE Process. We were later informed by the Tucson III committee that our workshop tied the record for most attendees for the entire conference. It was a wonderful to be with Rhea again and share our enthusiasm for EHE and the Network.

Rhea had a fantastic sense of humor; I still recall her laugh as I write these words. Her four or five cats gave her companionship and much joy. At the end of her life she would sit up in bed, with her cats frolicking and sleeping around her, surrounded with mountains of papers, books and journals. Her work never stopped. During her last years, Rhea, the editor-in-chief of the *Journal of the American Society for Psychical Research* guided me for five years to be the full time editor of that 100-year-old, peer-reviewed academic journal. While she was ill, Rhea continued to collect accounts, write emails, log information into her database and search for answers.

Rhea's best friend, Jean Spagnolo wrote me in 2015 about Rhea's NDE:

Rhea was in the hospital in Syracuse, NY after her accident. Many times I heard her telling people how when she went through the windshield of the car that she felt as if she were floating and thought she was dead.

The strange thing is that Rhea's father had a strict rule about letting anyone drive Rhea's car. To me she would often say that she wondered if she had been driving would the accident have happened and if so, would she have been killed like her colleague was.

I know that accident was the turning point in her life, as she said she was spared for some reason as she knows she was dead and floating in air for a time. She vowed to prove that ESP existed.[32]

A few months before her death, Rhea was awarded an honorary Ph.D. for her lifelong achievement with exceptional human experience in the field of transpersonal psychology from the Institute for Transpersonal Psychology (ITP), now called the Sophia Institute.

As Professor Charles Tart wrote in Rhea's tribute:

Today I was quite saddened to hear that Rhea White, friend and colleague, the recipient of an Honorary Doctorate from [ITP] last year, had died this morning. . . . We made Rhea very, very happy by recognizing her work with our Honorary Doctorate. . . .Rhea had been ill with a poorly diagnosed illness for several years now, having more and more difficulty breathing, but working as hard as she could on her EHE projects. She fell recently and broke her hip, but was eventually allowed to come home as her good friends would make sure she got the home care she needed in her recovery. As one of my correspondents put it, ". . . she was 'Rhea' to the end, doing what she wanted to do, feeling happy ('the best time of her

---

[32] Personal communication, e-mail from Jean Spagnolo, 4/16/2015.

life,' as she put it, all those later years when she was exploring consciousness, dreams, EHEs, including the end, and even as in age she grew older, ... her spirit thrived more and more, lighter and lighter)." If any of you had students who worked with her EHE material you might want to let them know. . . . Charley [33]

I called her the day before she passed away, my last call, and told her I loved her. She quipped back to me, "I know that, Suzanne!"

Rhea White was a phenomenon to all who knew her. She was herself, an Exceptional Human Experience. Besides sharing her story, I hope you can see the parallels to the overall EHE Process in this brief chapter. After her NDE, Rhea talked about it to anyone who would listen to a story about "floating" and "being dead." Without a doubt, Rhea's experience was real to her, so much so she totally shifted her life's direction and goals. It seems that because Rhea was catapulted directly into Stage 4: the Experiential Paradigm with her NDE, she would spend little time in Stage 3: Between the Worlds. Rhea in her later years wrote:

Putting exceptional human experiences at the forefront of our lives, both personal and professional, may be our best chance to save ourselves and our endangered world. This is the legacy I would like to leave for future generations. It is an outgrowth of my own

---

[33] Website: www.ehe.org front page

experiences in the 1950s that had to wait until I reached my 60s before I could begin to be able to realize them, even though they had been with me throughout my life. And the main reason I had the courage to become a heretic in an already heretical discipline was *my age*. I realized I would not live forever, and if I was ever going to apply what I have experienced and learned, I had better start right away and do the best I could in the time that remains with me.[34]

      Now, certainly we don't all have an NDE that includes an otherworldly voice and a feeling of bliss such as Rhea had with hers. However, I'll bet we all have had at least one meaningful coincidence or déjà vu or vivid dream that amazed us—caused us to question. *Exceptional experiences are sprinkled throughout our lifetimes, ready to be picked like fresh fruit.* It is up to us to become aware of them, pick them, make them our own.

      By now you have already selected at least one EE or EHE that moved you to explore more. In the next chapter, I will guide you through your own discovery process and writing your first EHE account. Then, in that same chapter, I will help you grow your EHE account(s) and get started writing your own EHE autobiography. There is nothing too demanding about writing your EHE accounts and EHE autobiography—it is fun,

---

[34] White, Rhea. The Aftereffects of My NDE, EHE: Background Papers I, 1994: New Bern, NC; p.136-137.

insightful, and can be an exceptional human experience all its own!

Chapter 9
Your Own EHE Autobiography

The very act of putting your experience to paper (or the computer) allows you to *go into the experience* like you have never done before. It is a odd thing: When we are thinking about something in our heads, we tend to use the same processes again and again, turning the experience around in the same ways and repeating similar patterns. Yet, it really does not seem to move us any further, as said in the familiar quip defining insanity: *Doing the same thing over and over again, expecting different results.*

However, when we take the time to relax, open up to new awareness (See Chapter 2 for more inspiration) and just go with the flow of writing, we often discover we have written something outside of our usual stuck thinking. The *inside* of us, our subconscious mind, gets a chance to speak, so to speak, when we are writing in the flow. Some people will call this an EE of automatic writing—we are awake and aware at that time at a different level of awareness not usually found in our day-to-day strivings.

Long-forgotten memories may sift through. Perhaps they were incubating in the background for years and you will now be better able to release them when you put pen to paper. I recommend pen and paper for writing any EHE accounts, including your autobiography because, especially when I first wrote mine years ago, I found that this kind of writing is an intimate time with my more-connected Self. I learned I had the capacity to reach inside deeply, as well as outside of the box of everyday static-and-noise life concerns.

Of course you have choices in writing process. There are no hard or set rules. It is a fun thing to do. You may want to simply reach into your memory and go for the full EHE autobiography because you have already identified your EHE process and experiences. Or, you may wish to expound on one exceptional experience to show how you potentiated it. Another way might be to write a series of EEs/EHEs and group them in clusters of types or, if you find it easier, write about them in chronological order. The key with the chronological presentation, however, is you may find the process or the Aha! moment does not come at the time of the actual experience you are writing about. In that case, you may want to list your experiences on paper first and then look at how they cluster. Or perhaps you may now see how they changed your life and path. You may then wish to select an overarching theme to present: Is it the types of experiences that moved you, or is it the EHE Process that you found within those experiences that moved you, or do you simply want to recall and write about your EEs/EHEs?

Following any and more of the above suggestions will get you going toward an essay that is uniquely yours!

Let's begin with writing an EE/EHE account. I had previously written the following article for our www.ehe.org website. Below is a modified version:

The *key* to writing any Exceptional Human Experience (EHE) narrative is to *just simply begin*. Find yourself about thirty minutes of free time and a quiet place to collect your thoughts. Below are a series of steps with questions to ponder to get you started. Once you begin, you will find that remembering your story and writing it down from your point of view is immensely satisfying, even self-indulgent. Repeat as often as desired!

Your EHE narrative begins with an Exceptional Experience (EE). This may be from your earliest childhood, a more recent happening, the *only* one you can recall. It may be the one you feel most comfortable writing about or the most spectacular.

Steps and Questions to Ponder

1.   Select your EE. Bring it close to you from memory, letting it get richer, fuller, and vivid in your relaxed mind. Try to relive it or simply observe it, whichever is more comfortable.

2.   Then, begin jotting down a few reminder notes about that particular experience. Try to capture it, hold onto it in your mind while you take notes. Relive your senses and feelings of that time. What happened? Describe it. When did the experience take place? How long did it last? Where were you? Why did that particular experience impress you at that time?

3.   Next, go backward into time and try to remember the immediate circumstances leading up to that EE. What were you doing just beforehand? What mood were you in? How were you feeling? Who was with you, if anyone?

Describe your surroundings, your sense of time, and whatever else you can recall. What do you feel brought about the EE, if anything?

4.   Now, follow that one experience a bit further along and go forward in time. What happened? Soon after it was over, how did you feel? Were you exhilarated, frightened, awed, confused, or what? Try to express this feeling in words. Did this experience change or move you in any particular way?

5.   What did you do shortly afterwards? How did you react? Did you try to hide it as if nothing happened? Did you take it in stride? Did you tell anyone? If you shared it, when did you do it? *Did another person's reaction affect your own initial assessment and feelings*?

6.   Now, in hindsight of the whole situation, was the experience meaningful to you? Or, better forgotten? Did you learn anything from it overall? Did you gain any new insights or connections? Did this experience make a positive or negative difference in your life? Does it factor in any way in your life today? In summary, what did this experience show or mean to you?

Congratulations! You have just completed outlining your first EHE narrative account!

Please go on and begin writing your EHE account and see where it takes you. Once you have written your first account, you will probably want to explore other EEs in much the same way. Sooner or later you may discover that these experiences connect together in ways that you had not even considered before. This insight, sensing a connection across experiences, is, in itself, an EHE. It is here that you begin to recognize the larger tapestry of your life and you are well on your way to writing your full EHE autobiography.[35]

How did you do? Did the very act of remembering and writing your memories give you some feeling of accomplishment? To be able to bring back, retrieve something forgotten or to expound on something that has been in the forefront of your mind can be exhilarating in itself. Take time now to sense how your EEs/EHEs might connect. Because you now have the tool of understanding the incubation process, go ahead and mull over the experiences you have discovered and brought to light. Once you have caught even one connection, you might find surprising insight. This insight may of course hit you at an odd time, like when you are taking a shower or drifting off to sleep. In any event, honor these Aha! experiences, for they also are exceptional.

Now once you have written an EE/EHE account and want to explore more, then you are ready to look at writing your full EHE autobiography. For me, writing my autobiography was at first recording a series of EEs I had not yet potentiated. It was *only through the act of writing and reflecting on what I had written that I potentiated my EEs into EHEs.* I discovered more personal meaning, such as learning that clusters of synchronicities (for example, my "Blue Star")

---

[35] Portions taken from www.ehe.org: "How to Write an EHE Account: Getting Started," Suzanne V. Brown, 1997b; with permission from the Parapsychology Foundation.

served as guiding principles in my life. That was a huge discovery! I will bet that with every EHE account you write, you will want to go further and begin pulling what you have uncovered and discovered into a full EHE autobiography.

Depending on how much you go back and read, reflect and review, you will find you want to expand and grow your narrative. So, if you would like to begin with your EHE accounts and then go into the EHE autobiography, it will probably flow fairly easily. However, with the knowledge gained from writing your EHE account, you may want to start a fresh EHE autobiography and not stay with that original style. It is all up to you!

Here are some simple steps in writing the full EHE autobiography from another article I wrote for the ehe.org website:

Think of your life as a whole tapestry of inner and outer events. Now, as you concentrate on the inner, subjective side (not typical in our culture), an overall pattern may begin to emerge—one marked by threads of various personally meaningful events, feelings, connections, and outcomes. When you begin to tie together these colorful threads *based on meaning and meaningfulness* into your EHE autobiography, you gain a fresh perspective on your life. In essence, you gain a larger new vision of your uniqueness, your birthright, your full human potential. By more fully envisioning your personal tapestry, you can then begin to recognize your own pattern, and see how your life may play a significant part in an even larger overall tapestry. Perhaps, for the first time in your life, you may gain a greater appreciation of who you genuinely are, where you have been, and where you are going.

Note: the act of writing an EHE autobiography serves as a stimulus to the recollection of forgotten events. It may require several days or even weeks to recall many significant experiences. Once you are working on the EHE autobiography experiences will spring to mind even when you are engaged in other activities. You may see fresh connections between these experiences. These new insights may be incorporated into your EHE autobiography. The main "rule" to keep in mind is not to force the writing, yet be disciplined about it. Each time you sit down to it, reread what you have written. In doing so, new experiences and connections are likely to come to mind. [36]

Once you have gotten to a stopping point in writing your EHE accounts, or beginning your EHE autobiography, I have a few more suggestions for you:

1.   Take a break from the intensity and go back to the everyday for a while. You will have begun to acknowledge your own story and the importance of EEs/EHEs. You have now also set the "incubation/ background" process in motion, and further connections may come to you without conscious, directed effort.

---

[36] "Helpful Steps in Writing Your EHE Autobiography," Suzanne V. Brown, 1997c, www.ehe.org; with permission from the Parapsychology Foundation.

2.   Now pay particular attention to dreams, coincidences, intuitive hunches, and flashes of insight during this incubation time. Add these to your narrative. Anything and everything is pertinent at this point. Write them down, savor them, and try to understand what they are suggesting to you overall.

3.   After several days, during a quiet time, review all that you have written. Go ahead and write add-ons to your overall narrative, paying special attention to the similarities, the connections, and also to the contrasts and shadings.

Remember that the EHE autobiography is an *evolving* narrative, based on those experiences that promote awe, meaning, and wonder. Put your story aside for a while and come back to it again, and then again for new insights. In this ongoing process of turning our life tapestry innerside-out, you will discover your deeper nature, your purpose, your connections, and begin to find your way back to the tapestry of All-Life. Do not set a limit as to how long it will take to write it, but work at it as time permits, until you feel it is "done for now." You will recognize a stopping point and at that point, you have created your own work of art.

I encourage you to write at least one EHE account or two to get started. I believe you will get caught in the flow of writing and want to continue. It is simply a matter of getting started with about twenty to thirty minutes—similar to taking time to journal your thoughts, ideas and feelings.

EVERYBODY'S EXCEPTIONAL, INCLUDING YOU!

The EHE Process has been discussed in depth and is a major focus of this book. Writing your EHE autobiography is another process as well. *I submit because we are continuing to grow, develop and evolve within the EHE Process, we are in the very midst of an overarching, life-evolving creative process.* In the next section, I will share some concluding thoughts regarding EHEs and how they may relate to not only our personal Journey Homeward as an individual, but also to an overall, evolutionary Journey Homeward for Humankind.

Suzanne V. Brown

Chapter 10
EHE—Humankind's Evolutionary Process

Everybody's Exceptional, Including You! revealed that exceptional human experiences (EHEs) are personal, life-changing occurrences that shift the way we understand ourselves and envision the world. We learned that an exceptional human experience is the result of potentiating an original exceptional experience (EE). An exceptional experience may be any odd, unusual, anomalous, downright weird or out-of-this-world event that sets you on a unique quest to learn more about it and its meaning. That quest for meaning and understanding was described in detail as the five-stage EHE Process. In the course of advancing through the stages of the EHE Process, we discover the More we are and a New Way of Being in the World.

I propose that when we reach this point, we have discovered not only the More we are but also our life's purpose and meaning—we've evolved toward our intended self who remembers who we actually are. We have evolved toward our Divine Self. This statement above is powerful! Take a moment to reflect on it. Those of you who have worked with me through *Everybody's Exceptional, Including You!* understand just how much larger our lives can be when we potentiate even the simplest déjà vu or synchronicity. Those of you who have moved through the EHE Process in questioning your experiences may now have discovered how they are *calling you toward something bigger* than the concerns of the little ego self. You find you are in the midst of your Journey Homeward. This awesome, yet humbling awareness comes as a result of paying attention to your EEs and EHEs. I believe these discoveries are in our lives to move us forward toward recognizing and remembering our Journey Home.

Sometimes when we potentiate our EEs into EHEs, we are overwhelmed with new insight. Fresh understandings may stimulate us all at once. Being overwhelmed can be an aftereffect of a powerful EE/EHE and the overarching Process. At this juncture, it is important that we keep our feet on the ground, aware of the roadmap challenges for each stage. If your insights are inundating you, it can be important to seek out a reputable professional counselor for a time who understands "spiritual awakening," "spiritual emergence," "transcendental experiences" and/or the EHE Process, including the value of self-discovery within an overall life-shifting paradigm. For me, I was guided to a remarkable therapist, who did not belittle my EEs and EHEs. Instead, he allowed me to explore them in depth and led me to realize for myself their significance. A thought here: Your counselor or therapist should allow you to find answers for yourself.

Once you have begun your Journey toward wholeness, the world will open up to you. As discussed In Chapter 2, you will find you are in the flow of enriching life events. While I cannot speak to you individually, these are indeed the findings Rhea and I found in our analysis of the EHE accounts and autobiographies. Many EHEers wrote that they discovered or remembered their reason to be on Earth at this time.

In my case, I was initially flooded with my experiences. For example, I thought I was destined to be a healer; even to heal others at a distance. Literally. A few more decades of experiences have gone by, with insights growing and shaping my understanding of "healer" into a larger framework. Today I see that I can use my writing as a gift to help others learn for themselves. Your exceptional experiences, too, canl largely shape your destiny—they are more than simply isolated wow-wee events. And, as we discover the More we are, we understand, over time, the enormity of our responsibility to live as we have been led by those very experiences. This EHE Process underscores our personal, overarching, developmental odyssey. We come to see we are not only growing; we are *evolving* in the truest sense of the word.

To "evolve" means "to develop something gradually, often into something more complex or advanced, or undergo such development." [37] *We EHEers are that "something." We are changing and developing into more complex or advanced beings*.

Recall how Dick Richardson in Chapter 7 "heard" in his1963 music enveloping, cosmic-type of EHE that "something out there is in need"? It would take him two decades of questioning, exploration and another powerful EHE before he began to understand the depth of meaning in those words. Dick would spend the rest of his life

---

[37] Encarta Dictionary: English (North America).

as a volunteer to help others potentiate their own experiences and seek their own truth. With Dick's personality, his statements were strong and absolute. He stated his thoughts passionately because he was adamant that others think for themselves—seek and find their own reality without the beliefs and authority of an outside influence. Bear in mind that Dick considered himself the "guru buster."

Personally, I suggest that what is in need is "all things," including humankind and Beyond. Dick was gave me an early reminder that not only do our EHEs shift our consciousness into a new worldview and awareness, they have the potential to propel us toward becoming our more connected Universal Self—or as Rhea put it, we become in touch with our divinity. Dick further stated that those who undergo the EHE Process are actually an advanced human species—*homo esophicus*, a term he created meaning "New Wise Man."

I am intrigued and wonder about this New Wise Man. Dick considered *homo esophicus* to be a hybrid human—evolving beyond our current classification of *homo sapiens*. I, too, have had several shifts of consciousness over my years where I felt as if I am from somewhere else not of this Earth. I wonder whether it is a remote DNA memory. Recall my experiences with other beings when I was quiet at home in my easy chair, waiting for a friend in the mid-1980s [Chapter 3], and when I was a little girl, skipping to the grocery store [Chapter 7]. On both occasions I sensed I was one of "them" and "they" were at "Home." Neither time has ever been forgotten. Today I realize they apparently led me to becoming more open about my EHEs and my Journey.

A few years before he passed away, Richardson emailed me, "Life is not about fulfilling oneself, but about fulfilling LIFE—an alien concept to that of *homo sapiens,* who themselves are alienated from life by their own way of life."[38] Take some time to ponder this statement. There is a lot to it. Once we get away from our instinctual drives to fulfil egoistic needs, we wake up to Stage 5: A New Way of Being in the World.

In pursuing our Journey, we uncover a paradox: The EEs/EHEs lead us to our Universal Self, and our Universal Self is known through our EEs/EHEs. It works both ways. If we are indeed evolving toward a new species, our EEs/EHEs are prodding us forward to re-member. In other words, we are gathering the parts of us that seem at first unconnected, then reconstructing the whole of who we are authentically. This reconstruction of the Universal Self happens naturally when we pay attention to our experiences and potentiate them.

Sharing further, Dick defined this species as, "Man who walks the face of the Earth, knowing what he is, where he came from, and why, and then fulfils Life incarnate." [39]

By bringing in Dick's hypothesis, I wanted you to see just how EHEs, when potentiated over the years and gathered into a new worldview, have the capacity to totally shift us in our everyday thinking, feeling and sensing. As I have written in

---

[38] Richardson, Dick, personal communication, August 9, 2009.
[39] IBID

my first two books, *Life is our spiritual Journey back Home.*[40] It is still a true statement today.

Life prompts us to explore our odd and weird occurrences. In fact, I believe Life compels us at this time to wake up and pay attention. We as individuals and as a species are at a critical juncture. I wonder aloud whether there is a Stage 6 and beyond in our EHE Process. Not only can we find a new way of being in the world, we are in touch with the Divine. For our purposes, "Divine" simply means we are in touch with our sacredness in a spiritual, universal sense, and not ascribing to any particular religion or belief system.

Whether you agree that we are evolving toward a new hybrid species or connected to the great Beyond, or made of stardust, we can agree we are moved to find our personal More. Exceptional experiences, when potentiated and revisited over time as EHEs, have the capability to re-mind us toward our higher purpose. To pursue and realize our calling is our spiritual quest for the Holy Grail within.

As Rhea writes, "Exceptional human experiences pull us out of a life of boredom and disconnection into a life of meaning and connection. We have to learn to honor these experiences and let them into our lives. When a sufficient number of people do that, the larger story will emerge. . . .The story of each human will

---

[40] *Blue Hills Diary: Mystical Journey into Mania*; Chipmunka Publishing, 2012. *Nightmares & Bliss: Journeys into Bipolar Mania*; Chipmunka Publishing, 2014

be the story of humankind."[41] Rhea's statement here is important for us to realize. She reminds us that humankind's story told over the ages is the result of each of our stories. I agree that when a critical mass of people on this Earth is awakened by their EEs/EHEs, our combined human story will change. No longer ruled by limitations—such as the prevailing scientific model—humankind will remember its universal, sacred Self.

All our experiences come together as a connected, colorful thread found deep within us as we continue to weave and tailor our tapestry of Life. Yes, the EHE Process is never-ending; yet, at some point you will have discovered the meaning of your universal Self. The search for meaning of the EE began our Journey. The search for meaning allows us to uncover that "something" we knew was within us, yet could not quite put our finger on. That, my friend, is your touch with sacred, with the Divine.

Life is our Journey back Home. During the course of this Journey, I trust you will have discovered your own answers and uncovered your own sacredness. Exceptional experiences and exceptional human experiences have that very power. Dig into life now—explore the More you are. You, too, are needed to add to the critical mass of EHEers who will lead us all Homeward, one EHEer at a time. Thank you!

---

[41] White, Rhea. Brief Overview of Exceptional Human Experiences. EHE; Background Papers I. The EHEN. Copyright 1994. The Parapsychology Foundation, with permission.

Suzanne V. Brown

Acknowledgments

Over the past decades I have been asked countless times to write a book on exceptional human experience and my work with Dr. (hon.) Rhea A. White, founder of the Exceptional Human Experience (EHE) Network. When Rhea asked me to join her as Vice President, Director of Research and Theory Development, I was thrilled! I met with her at her home in New Bern, NC and she introduced me to her dear friend from Penn State college days, Mrs. Jean Spagnolo. I have spoken with Jean on the phone and shared many emails, until her recent passing in 2016. I am grateful for her enthusiasm, suggestions and blessings for *Everybody's Exceptional, Including You!*

After Rhea passed away, her long-time friend and supporter Lisette Coly, President of the Parapsychology Foundation (PF), agreed to take on Rhea's journals, newsletters, and databases, as well as continue to maintain the www.ehe.org website under PF's watch. Lisette has generously allowed me to use quotations from EHE articles, writings from our ehe.org website and the two appendices with PF's kind copyright permission. Thank you for your support, permissions and sharing this Journey, Lisette.

Another big thank you goes to Margaret Harrell, my email friend since our early EHE Network days in the 1990s. Margaret offered many helpful editing and conceptual suggestions which made this book much more readable. Thank you, Margaret, for all your conscientious work on *EEIY* while you were finalizing your own most recent book about your own EHEs, worldwide travels and liaisons with "outlaw writers," *Keep This Quiet! IV.*

When I first read Dick Richardson's EHE autobiography about his cosmic EHE, we became close email friends "over the pond." I learned from him the best we can share is our truth. Dick was the "guru buster" extraordinaire. He told me to leave a legacy with my writings for future generations. Sadly, Dick passed away in 2013. Thank you, Dick for all your writings, dedication and encouragement, as especially recognized in Chapter 7 and Chapter 10.

Many thanks to my special dear friend, Nancymarie Jones, who also left this earth too soon in 2012. Nancymarie was a powerful EHEer as well as a creative artist. She provided the cover art for my first two memoirs. *Blue Hills Diary: Mystical Journey into Mania* and *Nightmares & Bliss: Journeys into Bipolar Mania.* Thank you, Nancymarie, for your love, sharing and gifts.

Special thanks go to my Aunt Marian Beckman for her encouragement throughout the writing and publishing of all three of my books. We have spent countless hours over lunches and her kitchen table discussing formatting, style, readability and marketing approaches. You continue to support and brighten my days with your thoughtful questioning and sharp mind.

Along the way, many people have encouraged me to keep writing, providing emotional support for me, including neighbors Lawrence (Larry) and Lori, and colleagues, Ellen, Janet, William, Charlotte, Sara, and Karen. I especially want to recognize my psychologist, Dr.

EVERYBODY'S EXCEPTIONAL, INCLUDING YOU!

Brian Monteleone of Charlotte, NC, who spent eight years helping me turn forward, away from my fearful, painful past. He gently asked the tough questions that would lead me to listening to my more connected Self. I also want to thank my Arizona psychiatrist, Dr. Gurvinder Sodhi, for listening to me with a sincere heart and thoughtful, perceptive mind.

Special thanks go to Jason Pegler and Andrew Latchford of Chipmunka Publishing for believing in me and the value of my works, and for publishing all three of my books.

And from the depths of my soul, I thank all people who have undergone Exceptional Experiences, and decided to pursue and potentiate them, rather than dismiss or fear them. As we evolve, we are building a new world together. Blessings on your Journey Homeward!

Suzanne V. Brown

APPENDIX I

A Dictionary of EHE-Related Terms: An Experiencer's Guide

Rhea A. White
Suzanne V. Brown
Original copyright © 2000.
Copyright © 2001 EHE Network, Inc.

Copyright © 2007 The Parapsychology
Foundation, Inc., with permission

These are terms that we have devised in an effort to clarify the nature of exceptional human experiences (EHEs). This dictionary also includes some psychological or sociological terms we have adopted and use in a special way in connection with EHEs.

Aftereffects. The immediate and long-term behaviors, feelings, meanings, insights, realizations, and outcomes described by EHEers as a result of reflecting on and potentiating their experiences. Different types of EHEs may yield similar aftereffects and outcomes, such as empathy, inner peace, courage, changed identity, and sense or even conviction of interconnectedness.

Anomalous Experience (AE). An experience that cannot be explained in terms of physics, psychology, sociology, or other accepted discipline is considered anomalous. Often it is dismissed by recourse to various applications of the law of parsimony. Failing that, it is passed off as likely due to chance or possibly as a delusion of the experiencer's or even as a hoax. Our position is that the "prove it or forget it" approach either dismisses an anomalous experience on the one hand, or whether or not it is published, files it in a drawer or cabinet, so to speak, on the other. There is usually no interest evidenced in the potential meaning of the experience because until it is proven that it actually happened, there is no point in looking for its meaning. Our view is that if the experiencer is left with a feeling that there is meaning hidden somewhere in the experience, it is worth taking the time and trouble to try to draw out that meaning and see where it leads even if it is not possible to rule out all counterhypotheses. We think it is likely that the basic meanings revealed by these experiences, once they become potentiated into EHEs, is the key to the evolution of consciousness and also to saving planet Earth because of the types of changed consciousness that are associated with EHEs.

Anomaly of Personal Experience (APE). An anomaly of personal experience is a first-time experience. Because it is the first of its kind and often unexpected, it can be as mind-boggling as any genuine anomalous experience. Imagine what the natives thought when they first saw Columbus's ships—they could not recognize them as ships, for they had no words or concepts for such large objects floating in the water. They seemed like great sea beasts. Or take runner Mike Spino's college training run when he reached a speed far beyond any he had known. Although initially he didn't think he could keep up with the 6-mile schedule his coach had set for him, by the second mile he felt he was going so fast he felt that he must have be cheating somehow. "It was like getting a new body that no one else had heard about" (Spin, 1971, p. 224). When it was over and his coach told him his running time was phenomenal when matched against his past marks, Spin says he couldn't even speak "because for awhile I didn't know who I was. Was I the one who had been running or the ordinary Mike Spin? … I sat down by the roadway and wept" (p. 225). Having glimpsed his "larger" self by means of this anomaly of personal experience, Spin's life course was set. He has devoted his life to practicing and teaching spiritual running. (Quoted from M. Spin, "Running as a spiritual experience." In Jack Scott [Ed.], *The Athletic Revolution* [pp. 222-225]. New York: Free Press, 1971.)

Experiences playing golf were among the seminal EHEs that led me (Rhea White) to the concept of exceptional human experience. Spin did not break the mile record in his run. I did not break any records in golf—except my own. But that is what an anomaly of personal experience is: seeing, thinking, doing, hearing, feeling, sensing something you know you personally have never experienced before, even though many others have. It can make you feel very alone and also very special. In a society where people tend to want to be like others only better, such experiences give one a glimpse of what it means to be individual and unique.

Of course, there are anomalies of experience that hold for the entire human species. Any time a world record is set in sports or a new theory in physics is set forth that meets the tests set by the theorist's peers or a new invention comes into the world, there is "something new under the sun." Imagine the awe and wonder when the electric light was invented! Anomalies of personal experience, whether they are individual firsts or firsts for the species, can be powerful exceptional human experiences because they open mind, spirit, and body simultaneously.

Classes of Experience. We have identified nine general classes of Anomalous, Exceptional, and Exceptional Human Experiences (which one it is depends largely on the degree of meaning inherent in the experience and the extent to which the experiencer can realize it). They are called Death-Related, Desolation/Nadir, Dissociative; Encounter, Exceptional Human Performance/Feats; Healing, Mystical, Peak, and Psychical Experiences. (Each is defined separately here.)

Concomitants. These are physical, physiological, psychological, and spiritual secondary qualities, facets, and characteristics of experiences reported by EEers and EHEers about their experiences, which go beyond simply labeling the type of experience. Different concomitants. (Examples are time slowing down or seeming to stop, scalp tingling, mental clarity, vivid imagery, electrical effects, unconditional love.)

Death-Related Experience. The common denominator of these experiences is death. Included are experiences in which there is a sense of a separation of the physical from the nonphysical self, particularly occurring prior to, during, or after your own or another's death, and memories of being between lives or before a new birth. Also included are encounters with persons or animals known to be dead or claiming to be so, some verifiable, some not; or from persons or animals who have died but the experiencer was ignorant of that fact when the deceased were "seen." This group also includes experiences of dying or actually being "dead" medically as in near-death experiences, as well as strange experiences associated with the moment of death, such as clocks stopping and pictures falling as a person is dying at a distance, and after death, such as various forms of apparent communication with the dead, involving seeing, hearing, smelling, and touching.

Depotentiation. Used in connection with exceptional experience, this term refers to various ways in which an experiencer goes out of the way *not* to potentiate the meaning of his or her experience . There are many ways of doing so. Some of these are belittling it, denying it, repressing it, making fun of it, or not dealing with the fears it may initially arouse. In effect, the experiencer creates a narrative about the experience that distances it from him- or herself by putting the experience down in some way. Maslow's word for this is *desacralizing*. The opposite happens when an experiencer potentiates an exceptional experience into an exceptional human experience by realizing its hidden meaning. See also **Potentiation**.

Desolation/Nadir Experience. Marghanita Laski in her book *Ecstasy* (Indiana University Press , 1961) discusses desolation experiences as the opposite of ecstatic or peak experiences. Maslow, however, sees desolation/nadir experiences on the same continuum as peak experiences and as involving an interrelationship between light and dark. In Yin-Yang symbolism, one is constantly becoming more while the other becomes less. It has been my experience (White) that experiences of great desolation may precede peak experiences, though it may take some period of time for this to happen. In a sense, feeling desolate puts you in touch with the depths and heights of self unguessed in ordinary life the same way that a peak experience does. Desolation and nadir experiences can also be seen as a stage in a developmental growth process, as when the dark night is viewed as an integral part of the mystical process of becoming one with the divine. Also, experiences of desolation and nadir experiences are often associated with disaster, abuse, life-threatening illness, and devastation, which in turn can trigger exceptional experiences and often come to be viewed later as saving graces. There are several examples of this in the section on EHE Portraits. In any case, desolation and nadir experiences are associated with EHEs, and some serve as direct triggers of EEs/EHEs. Some research on this has been carried out and has been abstracted in our journal, but much more work needs to be done.

Dissociative Experience. Experiences in which the experiencer is not in his or her daily frame of consciousness when the experience occurs, as in automatic writing or channeling or dowsing, primarily because he or she has induced the altered or dissociated state in order to increase the likelihood that an exceptional experience will occur.

Double Vision. The experience of being able to identify and see as if from within at least one other worldview than that of the mainstream dominant culture. Double vision confers an acuter awareness of and more objective comprehension of the limitations of the accepted worldview than is available to those who accept its reality unconsciously and unthinkingly.

EE *see* **Exceptional Experience**

EE Account. A relatively short written essay/report describing a personal EE, the circumstances under which it occurred, and the concomitants of the experience, but with little or no attempt to look beyond the experience to its meaning and significance. Often the experiencer will volunteer that it is the only experience of its kind that they have ever had. Some people report having had only one EE, whereas others report having several. Some even say it was the most important experience of their lives, but they rarely elaborate on why. From our viewpoint, that is the most important aspect of the experience. Written correctly, an account should contain as many details as can be recalled about what happened that was objectively observable as well as what they experienced subjectively, whether it be thoughts, physiological responses such as goosebumps or feelings of the numinous or uncanny, and what they think is the significance of the experience. If the experiencer has no idea, the account should state this.

EEer *see* **Exceptional Experiencer**

EHE *see* **Exceptional Human Experience**

EHE Account. A report of an EE that either immediately or subsequently, spontaneously or through attention and effort, proved to be a life-changing experience for the individual. Not only is the experience described in detail, including the circumstances and subjective aspects of the experience, but also its aftereffects. In order to be an EHE account, the aftereffects must involve a change in the experiencer that entails the realization of more of his/her human potential than ever before. Usually the person feels prompted to change his or her life in some way and sees him or herself and reality in a new way. This should be described in detail, relating the changes to the experience where possible.

EHE Autobiography. An EHEer's in-depth written essay/report and personal story in which his or her life is not told primarily in terms of objectively verifiable events but by her or his exceptional experiences, especially those that became EHEs. Moreover, the writer makes a conscious effort to draw an invisible inner line connecting the experiences even if they were very different and occurred several years apart and on the surface were not unconnected. This exercise not only can lead to insight, self-discovery, and meaning, but it can connect life experiences in a meaningful way such that a sense of life purpose and the potential for self-actualization is glimpsed or more deeply affirmed. It can also lead to the recollection of other EE/EHEs one has forgotten. In an EHE autobiography, you try see the line of your life as exclusively as possible in terms of your exceptional experiences. You must try to think of your life not as a chronological series of events, activities, and relationships, but as a number of subjective experiences that are likely to relate to the basic meaning and intention of your life.

EHE Chain. Once an experiencer knows what types of EEs/EHEs he or she has had and learns the history and lore of that experience or those experiences and meets others who have had the same or similar experiences, a sense of connection develops. First, it centers on those ahead of you who become your teachers and guides. Then, as you gain experience yourself, it extends backward to those new to the experience who depend on you for guidance and information.

It also stretches back in time to those experiencers who are no longer alive but whose writings or other communications still inform the living. Many experiencers feel the need to describe their own experiences for present and future generations, thus extending the chain into the future. This chain of people associated with a specific type or types of EE/EHEs is what we mean by the EHE chain. It is a term we do not often use in writing about EHEs, but it is a major aftereffect of some experiencers' EHEs. Parapsychologist William G. Roll has adopted the Iroquois Indian term *long body* and uses it for the sensory and nonsensory trail that follows a person through life on earth, becoming increasingly longer as he or she lives. It involves all that he or she has come into contact with physically and includes traces of its impact upon that person. This "long body" or patches of it is perceivable to psychics and specific memories are associated with certain objects the person used or loved and associations to it can be discerned via psychometry.

Similarly, the EHE Chain can be conceived as all of the experiencers back through history who have had a specific type of anomalous experience and realized its meaning for themselves and sometimes for others who did not have the actual experience. This chain can be drawn on by experiencers today and will be there for experiencers in the future. Although they may draw strength and wisdom from it in nonordinary ways, the record is also there in writings, published and unpublished, and more recently, audiotapes, videotapes, and now CD ROMs and web-sites. The realization of the existence of the chain to which each type of EHE you have had is a part provides a powerful timeless sense of connection with these others who have shared the same experiences you have, each in their unique ways and circumstances, even as yours is unique, but there is a large residue of sameness that remains. Many experiencers have died because of their experiences, and others have become famous because of them. Awareness of the EHE chain gives the experiencer a strong sense that there is a history here, and that he or she and others living now are continuing the chain so that those who will follow in the future will be able to draw upon it, at least for wisdom and moral support, and who knows, perhaps in more direct ways we cannot explain yet can imagine, feel, sense and benefit from.

EHE Cluster. It is not unusual for EEers or EHEers to have several different types of EEs/EHEs. However, in some cases people tend to have several experiences of the same or similar type. This is called an EHE cluster, because the same type of experience seems to cluster around the same experiencer. They can be looked at as a group of experiences encircling the experiencer, who is at the center. They may present different facets of viewing a given topic or component of the experiencer's personality or aspect of his or her life or they may connect various points of meaning not previously thought to be related. Or they may call attention, repeatedly, to things the experiencer has ignored, but as a result of the inexplicable cluster of experiences, it is no longer possible to ignore. There are other possibilities— each one tailored to the individual experiencer's situation.

EHE Interview. Interview with a person known to have had one or more EEs and/or EHEs about the details of their experiences and their aftereffects. The aim of the interview is to obtain information on as many as possible of the specific points listed under **EHE Account** and **EHE Autobiography**.

EHE Process. A sense of process can be conferred by EHEs, especially when inner and outer events come together in a meaningful way and over a period of time, thus indicating a graduated, evolving, evolutionary, internally reiterative series of stages that are initiated by EHEs. This eventually results in the sense that one is involved in an ongoing process that is happening both within and without and that is moving the experiencer in the direction of actualizing his or her human potential. Often it culminates in the creation of a **Project of Transcendence (PT)** and even in finding one's vocation and a sense of belonging. Our research accounts suggest five (5) stages may be involved: Initiatory Experience, Search for Reconciliation, Between Two Worlds, In the Experiential Paradigm, and A New Way of Being in the World. The latter usually involves living out some aspects of some experiences in some way, as in a vocation or a **PT**. It is likely that highly advanced experiencers will encounter still other stages beyond. These still need to be mapped. (I, that is,

Rhea White, can only do so at second hand, as I have not gone beyond this point.)

EHEer *see* **Exceptional Human Experiencer**

Encounter Experience. The experiencer is confronted with something that is actually there but is awesome and wondrous, such as a high a mountain peak or a clock that stops at the moment someone at a distance dies, or is not supposed to be there, such as a UFO or a Marian apparition,

EP *see* Experiential Paradigm

Exceptional Experience (EE). An anomalous experience that has a personal appeal for the experiencer so that he or she cannot brush it away or forget it even though there may be a normal explanation for it, albeit one that does not convince the experiencer. The EE is the mid-stage between an anomalous experience or anomaly of personal experience and an exceptional human experience.

Exceptional Experiencer (EEers). An individual who has had any kind of EE.

Exceptional Human Experience (EHE). Umbrella term to cover those EEs for which experiencers have been able to potentiate their sensed but hidden meaning, consciously realizing it, sometimes after long work and hard effort, not without risks. Usually this realization results in a transformed identity, lifeview, lifeway, and/or worldview of the experiencer, at which point the EE becomes an EHE. The changes are in the direction of realizing/actualizing the experiencer's full human potential.

Exceptional Human Experiencer (EHEer). An individual who has potentiated several of his or her EEs, that is, realized the human potential implicit in each one. This, in turn, has or is or will transform his/her perspectives on self, life, and worldview.

Exceptional Human Performance/Feats. Activities that extend the limits of what a person has been accustomed to doing or that are beyond the reach of what humans are expected to be able to do. They can be anomalies of personal experience for the performer, or they can serve as encounter experiences for spectators, evoking feelings of awe and wonder. This is one reason sports events are so popular. For example, a TV commentator at the 100th U.S. Open Golf Championship, which was held in 2000, said that what was so exciting about the play of Tiger Woods was not simply the steadiness of his exceptional play but the fact that we have come to expect that at any given moment, we will witness him making shots no one has ever seen before or even conceived of trying, and succeeding superbly. This is an example of a vicarious EE engendered by watching an exceptional human performance. Maybe the older generations watching will never duplicate such feats, but for aspiring young golfers, Woods is setting new limits that they will attempt to surpass when they themselves join the ranks of professional players.

Experiential Paradigm (EP). A worldview that is based not on physical data and logic but on the sum total of one's EHEs. Its tenets must be experienced to be known. These experiences eventually lift a person into a whole new way of perceiving reality. He or she is no longer enmeshed in the old worldview but can see it as if from outside. At the same time, the EHEer is aware of being in a new worldview that is based on heart knowledge and inner being that rests on a personal sense of connection with the entire creation. *See also* **Plateau Experience.**

Healing Experience. Experiences of healing that are beyond the bounds of allopathic medicine or that can only be explained as spontaneous remissions as well as experiences that integrate and energize mind and soul to an extent the experiencer had not previously known.

Lifeview. An EHEer's personal realization of his or her place in the grand scheme of things. It is an outcome of the EHE process in which the experiencer realizes that he or she is connected with all life and has a unique viewpoint, contribution, and purpose in that scheme. Once this sense of connectedness becomes part of your daily experience, it ushers in a new way of viewing your life. You sense a continuity underlying your life from birth (and for some, before) to death (and sometimes after). You also come to think of your own life as part of the life of the planet Earth and all of existence from the beginning as well as that of the universe at large. This new view of your life that is engendered and informed by one or more EHEs is called a lifeview. It is similar to worldview, except the personal element is featured—your own individual place in the scheme of things—as part of the whole and as the whole in the part.

Lifeway. This a way of life or lifestyle adopted or created by an EHEer for purposes of living in harmony with the lifeview and worldview that he or she became aware of when the meaning of one or more EHEs was realized. EHEers learn to look for additional experiences, and with this increased attention they see more connections and come to feel as though they have found their path in life, that they are doing what they are "meant" to do in the way they were "meant" to do it. Similarly, by this stage they know other EHEers and are still more motivated to change their lives in ways these others have done in their own ways. Then it can be said that they have found their lifeway. In addition, to finding their unique way of being in the world, EHEers generally make life changes that are in line with ways of promoting health, the well being of other humans and other species, and the preservation of Earth.

Mystical Experience. An experience that connects the experiencer throughout his or her being with something previously considered to be other or outside oneself or even nonexistent, such as God or Goddess or the divine, but also it could be an animal, a neighbor, a field, or a place that somehow, as a result of the experience, feels like "home" or is identified with the experiencer in some way as if it were intimate and familiar. It could even be a criminal or a person previously considered to be an enemy. There is a pronounced sense of greater connection, sometimes amounting to union, with the divine, other people, life-forms, objects, or one's surroundings, up to and including the universe itself. A sense of ecstasy or of being outside of one's skin-encapsulated ego self, is often experienced.

Nadir Experience *see* **Desolation/Nadir Experience**

Narrative. A written or spoken telling of events to another from the narrator's individual perspective and the unique aspects of his or her experience. The reader or listener does not question the narrative. It is accepted and valued as it stands with the understanding that the story is colored, flavored, and generated from within the perspective of the narrator. Our research at EHEN often involves studying written narratives, such as the **EE Account**, **EHE Account**, and the **EHE Autobiography**.

From the experiencer's viewpoint, his or her account of an experience in effect is a narrative he or she both reports and creates. The narrator consciously and deliberately may start the tale by recalling an experience but after awhile, as he/she calls on heights and depths and even

consciousness states he or she is usually not in touch with, the tale can begin to take the narrator to new and sometimes unanticipated places in reality and in self. From the viewpoint of traditional scientists, this is fabrication, confabulation, tampering with "reality." From our perspective, which places the meaning of an experience first, it is part of the process of both reaching out to hidden meaning and letting the sometimes palpable sense of meaning provide the words, which consciously the experiencer does not have. In fact, one aim in narrating the experience is to end the narrative knowing more about self and reality, based on the experience, than the narrator did when he or she began. Experiencers can take an affirmative stance toward their experience or one of dismissal and denial. The former tend to potentiate the meaning of their experiences, whereas the latter tend to depotentiate their experiences and sometimes even themselves..
See also **Depotentiation; Potentiation**

The Other. An anomalous experience, whatever else it may be, is an encounter with the Other. This is a blanket term for anything considered to be different from or alien to the perceiver or experiencer. The experiencer tends to not understand the Other because he or she can feel no empathy for or sense of unity with the Other. By granting at least a provisional reality to an anomaly, however, if it is a genuine EE eventually a sense of meaning will lead the experiencer on, and if it is potentiated and becomes an EHE, the experiencer will come to know what it is to embrace the Other, which now turns out to be his/her own self, plus more. In an EHE the experiencer not only discovers the More in the Other but also in him or herself.

Peak Experience. Term coined by Abraham Maslow for a wide variety of experiences whose core consists of those that are at the very limits of what Euro-American culture considers "normal." Most belong to the category of anomalies of personal experience rather than anomalous experiences. Although many of them are purely subjective, this category also includes many forms of exceptional human performance that are not considered beyond the bounds of possibility but that are unique to the experiencer. Maslow pointed out that many peak experiences are mystical experiences. Often they take the form of "personal bests" that extend the known limits of mental and physical apprehension and comprehension and execution as well as going beyond previous limits of emotional depths and heights. They also include "personal firsts" in the areas of thinking, feeling, knowing, learning, and performing for the first time. Also included are "normal" encounters with the exceptional such as with a holy person, a teacher, a mentor, or a charismatic individual, holy places, such as temples, mosques, cathedrals; or places associated with ancient events like the plains of Marathon, the fields of the Olympiad, the Great Pyramid, and the ruins of Mayan and Aztec temples. Most common, but not the least wondrous, is the experience of being in love and performing or being the recipient of or simply witnessing gratuitous acts of kindness and other altruistic behaviors. Running a sub four-minute mile and tying your shoelaces for the first time are both extensions of and enhancements of your being. Being carried away by music, rhetoric, reading, art, witnessing wondrous feats can all lead one to the brink of and sometimes over into an EHE. A person who extends the boundaries for the whole species, such as running the first four-minute mile or walking on the moon in some way immediately potentiates that act for the entire human species, at least those members who know about the feat. It becomes a part of our human potentiality, and realizing human potentiality is what EHEs are all about.

Plateau Experience. .Abraham Maslow identified a longitudinal form of peak experience, which he called a *plateau experience. I*n such experiences, what previously had been the "heights" or "peaks" of experience have become every day experiences, and they are experienced as very serene and over extended periods of time. Maslow wrote that in the plateau experience one perceives "under the aspect of eternity and become[s] mythic, poetic, and symbolic about ordinary things. ...There is nothing excepted and nothing special, but one lives in a world of miracles all the time" (p. 113; in S. Krippner [Ed.], 1972, *Journal of Transpersonal Psychology*, *4*, 107-120). Maslow observes that although the plateau experience includes elements common to peak experiences, such as "awe, mystery, surprise, and esthetic shock," they "are constant rather than climactic" (in Krippner, 1972, p. 113).

Note: It appears that Maslow's plateau experience in essence is similar to what we call living in the **Experiential Paradigm (EP)**, in which one becomes one with the flow of life, not separate from it. The term "plateau," however, connotes being on one level, whereas in the EP one is in touch with everything everywhere all at once, the fullness of being, which it seems to me (White), is a long-term multidimensional experience rather than a plateau. Nonetheless, it is clear in his definition of the plateau experience that Maslow was not referring to anything boring. It appears to be a nonlocal, nonlinear world, and not our accustomed linear one. Usual life has become the Tao, where Tao is the "EP" or the "plateau." It is also similar to David Bohm's *implicate order*.

Potentiation. This term, used in connection with exceptional experience, refers to the ability of an EE to potentiate higher human potential if the experiencer responds to it in an open, welcoming, curious, and inquiring manner with a view to understanding its meaning, thus "potentiating" the EE into an EHE by realizing the former's potential meaning. The opposite is depotentiation, in which one responds to an EE by ignoring, denying, minimizing, or rationalizing it away, and thus reducing it to an experience that can be dismissed more easily. *See also* **Depotentiation**.

Project of Transcendence (PT). After cultivating and nurturing EHEs, they may lead to a new way of being, living, and connecting in the world. This may lead to fresh insights concerning one's life purpose and "calling" that involve aspects that transcend the experiencer's ego and everyday activities and bestow a sense of grace and of doing and living as one is uniquely "meant" to do. Projects of Transcendence can be avocational, such as a specific art or craft or recreational activity (e.g., a sport), or they can be genuine callings, such as nursing, farming, studying marine mammals, veterinary work, or any number of old and new ways of making a living that is personally and cosmically meaningful. They are activities that extend over a period of time, possibly a lifetime, with built-in opportunities that enable the experiencer to grow more and give more back to life, which in turn is continually pushing the limits from within and without to new depths and heights of experience. This is because, in our view, it is the evolutionary impetus to growth and in humans, the extension of consciousness to new levels inwardly and outwardly that is at the base of EHEs.

These projects are almost always initiated by an EHE which, if assiduously followed, will lead, at the lower end, to engagement in a meaningful activity, and at the higher end, to a discipline that will fully engage the person over a long period of time, possibly a lifetime. During the course of the project the person becomes aware of a deep connection or even a oneness with a deeper self, other people, other life forms, the Earth, the Universe, and the sacred. As part of this ongoing process, more EHEs will likely be experienced.

These Projects of Transcendence have existed since earliest recorded times. Every one of the world's religions is a Project of Transcendence, as is every art and craft. A Project of Transcendence is usually initiated by a call to transcendence, or what used to be known as a calling, or sense of vocation. That call is itself a form of exceptional human experience. In the past the lore concerning each art or religious discipline was carried by institutions, whether they were monasteries, guilds, or schools. Within these institutions each person was likely to have a spiritual director, master craftsman, teacher, or mentor to offer guidance concerning their exceptional experiences. One of the best modern descriptions of these projects is *Inevitable Grace: Breakthroughs in the Lives of Great Men and Women: Guides to Your Self-Realization* by Piero Ferrucci (Tarcher, 1990). He describes the major ways of being in the world and finding unity, which he calls the ways of beauty, action, illumination, dance and ritual, science, devotion, and will.

We can learn about Projects of Transcendence in many ways. We can read or see films or listen to tapes or talk to persons who participate in certain activities we feel an affinity to which we are drawn. And we can read biographies and autobiographical writings about/by persons who have engaged in long-term activities that partake both of interactions with the world and with others in a way that involves "soulmaking." All these ways are both based on and can give rise to further EHEs that continue the process of becoming one with everything that is. They lead the experiencer into awareness of the **EHE process** and ultimately, the **Experiential Paradigm**.

Psychical Experience. Varied experiences whose core consists of a sense of personal interaction with other people, life forms, objects, and environments in ways that cannot be explained by known sensory, perceptual, or mechanical means, or by rational inference.

PT *see* **Project of Transcendence**

Worldview. The reigning authoritative perspective of how the world works as defined by the mainstream culture. Current Western culture is based on deterministic science and Judeo-Christian tenets. Issues of "common-sense" are based on these "realities." This view tends to see exceptional experiences at best as "anomalies," but the preferred is to explain them away. This is why such experiences force us to augment or even move beyond the current worldview so that it may incorporate more of what was once considered "other." The Experiential Paradigm, for example, is based on oneness and interconnectedness rather than separation. This promotes a reverence for all life rather than the view that any life form, including certain groups of humans, is open to exploitation, use, and abuse by other humans.

APPENDIX:
List of Potential EE/EHEs
Rhea A. White

Original copyright © 2000.
Copyright © 2001 EHE Network, Inc.
Copyright © 2007 Parapsychology Foundation,
with permission

Anesthetic Experience
Angel Encounter; *see also* Guardian Angel
Anxiety Dream; *see also* Night Terrors
Anomalous Weather Control *see* Weather Control,
Anomalous
Apparition; *see also* Collective Apparition
Apport
Archetypal Dream *see* Transcendent Dream
Archetypal Experience; *see also* Imaginal
Experience; Mythic Experience; Numinous
Experience
Architecture Experience; *see also* Holy or Power
Place Encounter
Art Experience
Astral Projection *see* Out-of-Body Experience
Aura Vision
Autism
Automatic Drawing
Automatic Painting
Automatic Speaking
Automatic Writing
Automatism; *see* Automatic Drawing; Automatic
Painting; Automatic Speaking;Automatic Writing;
Dowsing

Autoscopy *see* Bilocation; Double; Out-of-Body Experience;

Bardo Experience *see* Life Between Life

Being in the Zone *see* Zone Experience

Bilocation

Bioattraction

Blood Miracle, Witnessing

Bodily Functions, Exceptional Control of

Bodily Transformation

Border Crossing Experience

Breakpoint Experience

Breathing, Inner

Brownies Encounter

Burial Alive *see* Suspended Animation

Call case *see* Clairaudience; Voices, Hearing

Calling *see* Vocation, Sense of

Celestial Music *see* Transcendental Music

Cellular Consciousness

Channeling

Chaos Experience *see* Desolation/Nadir Experience

Charismatic Personality Encounter; *see also* Exceptional Person Experience; Holy Individual Experience

Charismatic Prophecy *see* Prophecy

Child Prodigies *see* Prodigies

Childbirth Exceptional Experience

Christos Experience

Clairaudience; *see also* Locution; Voice, Hearing

Clairvoyance; *see also* Mindsight Experience

Clairvoyant Diagnosis *see* Paranormal Diagnosis

Clock-Stopping

Coincidences, Striking; *see also* Serendipity; Synchronicity

Collective Apparition

Collective Consciousness *see* Human Species
Consciousness/Connectedness
Collective Unconsciousness *see* Human Species
Consciousness/Connectedness
Coma Experience
Conscious Dying
Contemplative Experience; *see also* Meditation
Experience; Prayer Experience; Recollective
Experience; Yoga Experience
Conversion
Cosmic Consciousness/Connectedness
Cosmology, Personal *see* Cosmic
Consciousness/Connectedness
Creative "Aha" or Eureka Experience; *see also*
Embodied Insights
Crop Circle Encounter
Cross Correspondence
Crystal-Gazing *see* Scrying
Cutaneous Perception
Dance Experience
Darshan Experience
Daydreaming
Death-Related Experiences (Class)
Death-Related Psychokinesis; *see also* Clock
Stopping
Deathbed Experience *see also* Near-Death
Experience; Non-Near-Death Experience; Peak-
in-
Darien Experience
Deathbed Observation/Encounter
Deceased Spirit Experience *see* After Death
Communication
Déjà Vu; *see also* Jamais Vu
Dematerialization; *see also* Materialization

Demonic Encounter; *see also* Evil Entity
Dermo-Optic Perception *see* Cutaneous Perception
Dermography *see* Skin-Writing
Desolation/Nadir Experience (Class); *see also* Post-Traumatic Stress Disorder; Spiritual Emergency
Diagnosis, Paranormal *see* Paranormal Diagnosis
Direct Drawing Experience
Direct Painting Experience
Direct Physical Phenomena
Direct Voice Experience
Direct Writing
Dissociative Experiences (Class)
Dissociative Identity Disorder *see* Multiple Personality
Distant Intercellular Interaction
Divination
Divine Healing *see* Spiritual Healing
Döppelganger *see* Double
Double
Double Vision
Double-Release Out-of-Body Experience
Dowsing; *see also* Map Dowsing
Drama Experience
Dream Helper
Dreambody Experience
Dream, Impactful; *see also* Anxiety Dream; Dream Helpher; Existential Dream; Lucid Dreaming; Psychic Dream; Transcendent Dream; Transformative Dream
Dream, Lucid *see* Lucid Dreaming
Drop-in Communicator
Drug Experience *see* Hallucinogenic Drug Experience

Dying, Conscious *see* Conscious Dying
Earth Experience *see* Planetary Consciousness
Ecstasy; *see also* Shamanic Ecstasy
Effortlessness
Eidetic Imagery
Electrical/Electronic Sensitivity, Paranormal; *see also* Street Lamp Interference
Electronic Visual Phenomena
Electronic Voice Phenomena (EVP)
Elongation
Elusivity
Emanation
Embodied Insight
Embodiment *see* Inscendence/Embodiment/Immanence
Emotions, Transcendental
Empathy
Encounter Experience (Class)
Encounter or T-Group Experience
Energy Experience
Enlightenment; *see also* God/Goddess Experience
Epiphany
ESP *see* Extrasensory Perception
Esthetic Experience *see* Art Experience
Eureka Experience *see* Creative "Aha" Experience
Evil Entity; *see also* Demonic Encounter
EVP *see* Electronic Voice Phenomena
Exceptional Human Experience (General Heading); *see also* Transpersonal Experience
Exceptional Human Performance/Feat
Exceptional Person Encounter; *see also* Holy Person Encounter
Existential Dream

Experience of the New *see* New, Experience of the

Extrasensory Perception (ESP)

Extraterrestrial (ET) Encounter *see* Alien Encounter

Faces, Paranormal *see* Imprints, Paranormal

Fairies, Encountering

Faith Healing

Falling Experience

Family Psi

Fantasy *see* Daydreaming; Imaginal Experience

Feats *see* Exceptional Human Performance/Feat

Feeling of Being Stared at *see* Remote Staring

Fire-Immunity

Fire-walking *see* Fire-Immunity

First Contact Experience *see* New, Experience of the

First-Time Experience; *see also* New, Experience of the

Flow Experience

Folk Entity Encounter

Foreknowledge *see* Precognition

Fortune-Telling *see* Divination

Gaia Experience *see* Planetary Consciousness

Galactic Consciousness

Geller Effect *see* Metalbending

Genius, Experience of

Ghosts *see* Apparition; Haunt; Poltergeist

Global Consciousness *see* Planetary Consciousness

Glossolalia

God/Goddess Experience

"Going Native" Experience

Grim Reaper Apparition

Group Bonding

Group Experience/Entity
Group Past Life Recall
Group Psi
Guardian Angel Encounter; *see also* Inner
Guidance Experience; Helper Experience; Inner
Helper Experience; Locutions
Guru Encounter *see* Holy Person Encounter
Hallucination; *see also* Eidetic Imagery
Hallucinogenic Drug Experience
Haunt
Haunting
Healing Approaches/Experiences; *see also* Faith
Healing; Intercessory Prayer; Paranormal
Diagnosis; Psychic Healing; Psychic Surgery;
Shamanic Healing; Shamanistic Healing; Spirit
Healing; Spiritual Healing;
Healing, Psychic *see* Psychic Healing
Healing, Shamanic *see* Shamanic Healing
Healing, Shamanistic *see* Shamanistic Healing
Healing, Spirit *see* Spirit Healing
Healing, Spiritual *see* Spiritual Healing
Health/Well-Being/Wholeness Experience
Hearing or Reading About EHEs of Others *see*
Vicarious EE/EHE
Heart Knowledge
Helper Encounter
Helper Spirit
Heteresthesia
Highland Sight *see* Second Sight
Hitchhiker, Phantom *see* Phantom Hitchhiker
Holy or Power Place Encounter
Holy Person Encounter; *see also* Exceptional
Person Experience; Marian Apparition
Homing Ability *see* Orientation

Human Magnets *see* Bioattraction
Human Species Consciousness/Connectedness
Human-Animal Interaction *see* Interspecies
Communication/Encounter
Human-Machine Interaction
Hyperacuity
Hypermnesia
Hypnagogic Experience
Hypnopompic Experience
Hypnosis-at-a-Distance *see* Suggestion-at-a-
Distance
I-Thou Experience
Idiot Savant *see* Savant Syndrome
Illumination; *see also* Creative "Aha" Experience;
Enlightenment; Koan
Imaginal Experience
Imaginary Companion
Imaginary World *see* Paracosm, Creation of
Immanence *see*
Inscendence/Embodiment/Immanence
Immersive Thrill Experience
Immortality Experience
Immunity/Invulnerability; *see also* Fire-Immunity
Imprints, Paranormal
Incendium Amoris
Incipient Manic Psychosis
Incorruptible Flesh
Incubus Experience; *see also* Old Hag Experience
Influenced Writing *see* Channeling; Automatic
Writing
Inner Breathing *see* Breathing, Inner
Inner Guidance Experience; *see also* Guardian
Angel; Inner Helper Experience;
Inner Helper Experience; *see also* Guardian
Angel; Inner Guidance Experience; Locutions;

Inner Movement

Inscendence/Embodiment/Immanence; *see also* Recollective Experience

Inspiration; *see also* Channeling; Creative "Aha" Experience;

Inspired Writing or Drawing *see* Automatic Drawing; Automatic Writing; Channeling;

Intercessory Prayer

Interspecies Communication/Encounter

Intuition

Invisibility *see* Dematerialization

Jamais Vu; *see also* Déjà Vu

Koan; *see also* Creative "Aha" Experience

Kundalini Awakening

Kything

Laughter, Inward

Laying on of Hands; *see also* Therapeutic Touch

Levitation

Life Between Life

Life Interconnectedness Experience

Life Review

Life-Changing Experience *see* Conversion; Exceptional Human Experience

Lifehoods, Experience of

Light Experiences

Light Beyond the Light Experience

Limerence

Liminal Experience *see* Border Crossing Experience

Limit Experience *see* Border Crossing Experience

Literary Experience

Locutions

Love

Lucid Dreaming

Luck; *see also* Serendipity
Luminous Phenomena
Lung-Gom-Pa Running
Macrocosm/Microcosm Experience
Magic/Sorcery
Magnified Vision
Map Dowsing
Marian Apparition *see* Holy Person Encounter
Martial Arts Experience
Materialization; *see also* Dematerialization
Meaningful Coincidence *see* Synchronicity
Meditation Experience
Mediumistic Experience
Memory, Exceptional *see* Supermemory
Memory, Transpersonal *see* Recollective
Experience
Metal Bending
Metanoia *see* Exceptional Human Experience
Microscopic Vision *see* Magnified Vision
Mind Over Matter *see* Psychokinesis
Mindsight Experience
Mineral-Human Experience
Miraculous Experience/Encounter
Mirror Vision
Missing Time see Altered Time Perception
Moebius Experience
Monition; *see also* Premonition
Multiple Personality
Muscle-Reading
Music Experience

Music of the Spheres *see* Music Experience
Music, Transcendental *see* Music Experience
Mystic Heat *see* Tumo
Mystical Experiences (General Class)

Mythic Experience; *see also* Archetypal
Experience; Imaginal Experience
NAD *see* Transcendental Music
Nadir Experience *see* Desolation/Nadir
Experience
NDE *see* Near-Death Experience
Near-Death Experience (NDE); see also Life
Review; Light Beyond the Light Experience; Non-
Near-Death Experience; Tunnel Experience
New, Experience of the; *see also* First-Time
Experience
Night Terrors; *see also* Anxiety Dream
Nightmare *see* Anxiety Dream
Noble Acts, Witnessing or Performing
Noetic Experience
Non-Near-Death Experience
Nonallopathic Healing *see* Healing Experiences
Nostalgia
Numinous Experience
OBE *see* Out-of-Body Experience
Object-Reading *see* Psychometry
Odor of Sanctity *see* Scent, Transcendental
Odor, Paranormal; *see also* Scent,
Transcendental
Odor, Transcendental *see* Scent, Transcendental
Old Hag Experience; *see also* Incubus Experience
Oracles *see* Oracular Experience
Oracular Experience
Orgasmic Experience
Orientation
Other, Experience of the; *see also* Double Vision*;*
"Going Native" Experience;
Otherworld Personal Future Experience
Ouija Board Experience

Out-of-Body Experience (OBE)
Outer Space Experience
Outsider Experience *see* Border Crossing
Experience; Double Vision; Other, Experience of
the
Panoramic Memory *see* Life Review
Paracosm, Creation of
Paranormal Diagnosis
Paranormal Electrical Effect *see*
Electrical/Electronic Sensitivity, Paranormal
Paranormal Faces *see* Imprints, Paranormal
Paranormal Healing *see* Psychic Healing
Paranormal Imprints *see* Imprints, Paranormal
Paranormal Odor *see* Odor, Paranormal
Paranormal Sound *see* Sound, Paranormal
Paranormal Touch *see* Touch, Paranormal
Paranormal Voice *see* Voice, Paranormal
Past-Life Recall
Peace Beyond Understanding
Peak Experiences (Class)
Peak Performance *see* Exceptional Human
Performance/Feats
Peak-in-Darien Experience
Performing/Witnessing Noble Acts *see* Noble
Acts, Performing/Witnessing
Perinatal Experience
Personal Best Experience
Personal Cosmology *see* Cosmic
Consciousness/Connectedness; Outer Space
Experience
Phantom *see* Apparition; Haunt
Phantom Hitchhiker
Phantom Phone Call
Photography, Paranormal *see* Psychic
Photography

Physiological Feats *see* Exceptional Human Performance/Feats (General Class)
PK *see* Psychokinesis
Placebo Effect
Planetary Consciousness; *see also* World-Wide Web Experience
Plant-Human Experience
Plateau Experience
Poltergeist Experience
Possession
Post Mortal Messages *see* After Death Communication
Post-Mortem Communication *see* After Death Communication
Post-Mortem Painting, Visions, Voices, Writing *see* After Death Communication
Post-Traumatic Stress Disorder *see* Spiritual Emergency
Prayer Experience; *see also* Contemplative Experience; Intercessory Prayer; Meditation Experience; Yoga Experience
Prebirth Experience; *see also* Life Between Life
Precognition; *see also* Premonition
Premonition; *see also* Monition
Prenatal Experience
Presence, Sense of *see* Sense of Presence
Presque Vu
Primal Life Experience; *see also* Life Interconnectedness Experience
Prodigies; *see also* Savant Syndrome
Prophecy Experience
Proxy Sitter Experience
Psi Experience *see* Psychical Experiences (Class)
Psi Timing

Psychedelic Drug Experience *see* Hallucinogenic Drug Experience
Psychic Dream
Psychic Experiences *see* Psychical Experiences (Class)
Psychic Healing
Psychic Imprint Encounter
Psychic Photography
Psychic Surgery
Psychical Experiences (Class)
Psychography *see* Direct Writing
Psychokinesis
Psychomanteum Experience *see* Mirror Vision; OracularExperience
Psychometry
Psychoneuroimmunology
Psychotherapeutic Breakthrough Experience
Psychotherapeutic Resonance
Qiqong Experience
Rainmaking; *see also* Weather Control, Anomalous
Rapport
Raps *see* Sounds, Paranormal
Rapture *see* Ecstasy
Reading While Asleep *see* Sleep Learning
Reciprocal Apparition
Recollective Experience
Recurrent Spontaneous Psychokinesis *see* Haunts; Hauntings; Poltergeists
Reincarnation Experience *see* Past Life Recall
Remote Staring
Remote Viewing
Rescue Circle
Resurrection After Death
Retroactive Psychokinesis

Retrocognition
Reunion Experience *see* After Death
Communications
Revelation
Rhabdomancy *see* Dowsing
Rhythmic Experience
Rock-Human Experience *see* Mineral-Human
Experience
RSPK *see* Recurrent Spontaneous Psychokinesis
Sacred Sites *see* Holy or Power Place Encounter
Sacred Silence
Sacred Stillness
Sacred Vision
Savant Syndrome; *see also* Prodigies
Scent, Transcendental; *see also* Odor,
Paranormal
Scrying
Séance Experience
Second Sight *see also* Clairvoyance; Extrasensory
Perception (ESP); Precognition
Self-Realization *see* Enlightenment
Sense of Presence
Sense of Vocation *see* Vocation, Sense of
Serendipity; *see also* Coincidences, Striking; Luck
Shamanic Ecstasy
Shamanic Experience
Shamanic Healing
Shamanistic Experience
Shamanistic Healing
Shamanistic Initiatory Crisis
Shared Anomalous Experience (e.g., *see also*,
Collective Apparition; Shared Dream)
Shout *see* Spirit Shout

Shouting *see* Spirit Shout
Sight, Second *see* Second Sight
Silence, Sacred *see* Sacred Silence
Sitter Group Experience; *see also* Séance Experience
Sitting *see* Séance Experience; Sitter Group Experience
Sixth Sense *see* Extrasensory Perception (ESP)
Skin-Writing
Slate Writing
Sleep Learning
Sleep Paralysis
Soothsaying *see* Divination
Sorcery *see* Magic/Sorcery
Soul-Retrieval
Soulmate Experience
Sound, Paranormal
Speaking in Tongues *see* Glossolalia; Xenoglossy
Species Consciousness *see* Human Species Consciousness/Connectedness
Spirit Guide
Spirit Healing
Spirit Photography
Spirit Shout Experience
Spiritual Emergency/Emergence Experience; *see also* Desolation/Nadir Experience; Shamanistic Initiatory Crisis
Spiritual Healing
Spontaneous Cures
Spontaneous Human Combustion
Spontaneous Remission *see* Spontaneous Cures
Stair Flying
Staring, Remote *see* Remote Staring
Stigmata
Stillness, Sacred *see* Sacred Stillness

Street Lamp Interference; *see also*
Electrical/Electronic Sensitivity, Paranormal
Sublime, Experience of the *see* Numinous
Experience
Suggestology *see* Accelerated Learning;
Supermemory
Supermemory; *see also* Accelerated Learning
Supernatural Assault *see* Incubus Experience
Surrender
Suspended Animation
Synchronicity
Synergetic Experience
Synergistic Experience *see* Synergetic Experience
Synesthesia
Table Turning *see* Sitter Group
Table-tipping *see* Sitter Group
Tears, Transcendental *see* Weeping,
Transcendental
Telekinesis *see* Psychokinesis
Telepathy
Teleportation
Telesthesia *see* Clairvoyance
Temperature Changes, Anomalous
Theophany
Therapeutic Touch
Thought Transference *see* Telepathy
Thoughtography *see* Psychic Photography
Token Object Reading *see* Psychometry
Touch, Paranormal
Trance Running *see* Lung-gom-pa Running
Transcendent Experience *see* Numinous
Experience; Mystical Experience; Peak
Experience
Transcendent Dream

Transcendental Emotion *see* Emotion,
Transcendental
Transcendental Music *see* MusicExperience
Transcendental Odor *see* Odor, Paranormal;
Scent, Transcendental
Transcendental Tears *see* Weeping,
Transcendental
Transfiguration

Transformative Dream
Transpersonal Experience
Transpersonal Memory *see* Recollective
Experience
Tumo Experience
Tunnel Experience
UFO Abduction Experience *see* Alien Abduction
UFO Encounter *see* Alien Encounter
Uncanny Feeling/Sense
Unitive Experience
Unorthodox Healing *see* Healing,
Experiences/Approaches
Vanishing *see* Dematerilization
Vertigo Experience; *see also* Immersive Thrill
Experience
Vicarious EEs/EHE
Virtual Transcendent Experience
Vision Quest Experience
Visionary Experience; see also Sacred Vision;
Vision Quest Experience
Vocation, Sense of
Voices, Hearing
Void, Experience of the
Walk-In Experience
Water Witching *see* Dowsing
Weather Control, Anomalous

Weeping, Transcendental
Wholeness *see* Health/Wholeness Experience
Wilderness Experience
Wonder, Experience of
World-Wide Web Experience
Xenoglossy, Recitative
Xenoglossy, Responsive
Yoga Experience; *see also* Contemplative
Experience; Meditation Experience; Prayer
Experience
Zero Ground Experience
Zone Experience

CPSIA information can be obtained
at www.ICGtesting.com
Printed in the USA
FSHW020530040419
56958FS